VOLUME 6

OLD TESTAMENT

THE NEW COLLEGEVILLE BIBLE COMMENTARY

DEUTERONOMY

J. Edward Owens, O.SS.T.

SERIES EDITOR

Daniel Durken, O.S.B.

LITURGICAL PRESS

Collegeville, Minnesota

www.litpress.org

Nihil Obstat: Reverend Robert Harren, *Censor deputatus.*
Imprimatur: ✠ Most Reverend John F. Kinney, J.C.D., D.D., Bishop of Saint Cloud, Minnesota, December 17, 2010.

Design by Ann Blattner.

Cover illustration: *Hear, O Israel—Deuteronomy* by Hazel Dolby. Copyright 2003 *The Saint John's Bible*, Order of Saint Benedict, Collegeville, Minnesota USA. Used by permission. Scripture quotations are from the New Revised Standard Version of the Bible, Catholic Edition, copyright 1989, 1993 National Council of the Churches of Christ in the United States of America. Used by permission. All rights reserved.

Photos: pages 23, 40, 60, 82, 98, Photos.com.

1   2   3   4   5   6   7   8   9

Library of Congress Cataloging-in-Publication Data

Owens, J. Edward.
    Deuteronomy / J. Edward Owens ; series editor, Daniel Durken.
        p.   cm. — (The New Collegeville Bible commentary. Old Testament ; v. 6)
    Includes index.
    ISBN 978-0-8146-2840-9
        1. Bible. O.T. Deuteronomy—Commentaries.   I. Durken, Daniel.   II. Title.

    BS1275.53.O94 2010
    222'.15077—dc22

                                                                        2009053788

CONTENTS

ABBREVIATIONS

Books of the Bible

Acts—Acts of the Apostles
Amos—Amos
Bar—Baruch
1 Chr—1 Chronicles
2 Chr—2 Chronicles
Col—Colossians
1 Cor—1 Corinthians
2 Cor—2 Corinthians
Dan—Daniel
Deut—Deuteronomy
Eccl (or Qoh)—Ecclesiastes
Eph—Ephesians
Esth—Esther
Exod—Exodus
Ezek—Ezekiel
Ezra—Ezra
Gal—Galatians
Gen—Genesis
Hab—Habakkuk
Hag—Haggai
Heb—Hebrews
Hos—Hosea
Isa—Isaiah
Jas—James
Jdt—Judith
Jer—Jeremiah
Job—Job
Joel—Joel
John—John
1 John—1 John
2 John—2 John
3 John—3 John
Jonah—Jonah
Josh—Joshua
Jude—Jude
Judg—Judges
1 Kgs—1 Kings

2 Kgs—2 Kings
Lam—Lamentations
Lev—Leviticus
Luke—Luke
1 Macc—1 Maccabees
2 Macc—2 Maccabees
Mal—Malachi
Mark—Mark
Matt—Matthew
Mic—Micah
Nah—Nahum
Neh—Nehemiah
Num—Numbers
Obad—Obadiah
1 Pet—1 Peter
2 Pet—2 Peter
Phil—Philippians
Phlm—Philemon
Prov—Proverbs
Ps(s)—Psalms
Rev—Revelation
Rom—Romans
Ruth—Ruth
1 Sam—1 Samuel
2 Sam—2 Samuel
Sir—Sirach
Song—Song of Songs
1 Thess—1 Thessalonians
2 Thess—2 Thessalonians
1 Tim—1 Timothy
2 Tim—2 Timothy
Titus—Titus
Tob—Tobit
Wis—Wisdom
Zech—Zechariah
Zeph—Zephaniah

The Book of Deuteronomy

The book of Deuteronomy has a profound influence on both Testaments. It forms the basis of what scholars call the Deuteronomistic History, which extends from Joshua to 2 Kings; in the prophetic literature Hosea and Jeremiah show its influence as well. Some influence is also seen in the Chronicler and Tobit. The New Testament cites or alludes to Deuteronomy over one hundred times, including words from the lips of Jesus (Matt 4:4, 7, 10; John 8:35). With great breadth the Deuteronomic tradition informs our understanding of the Scriptures and offers an abiding theological message to believers in every age. In sum, Deuteronomy is panoramic, offering a bird's-eye view of the saga of Israel and informing later Jewish and Christian traditions.

Deuteronomy is essentially a book of torah, i.e., instruction in life and faith for curse or blessing (29:20; 30:10; 31:26). Homiletically, it is a proclamation to be read aloud. Moses is presented as writing the instructions at the end, and his message is to endure as a proclamation in the assembly (31:9-13). This attitude reflects ancient literacy in which communication and understanding came more through the ear than the eye, even though the eye was a metaphorical window to knowledge (4:9).

The historical background of Deuteronomy

It is beyond the scope of this introduction to discuss at length the complex history and redaction (changes and additions by later authors) of Deuteronomy. Numerous books and articles are available on the subject. However, a few observations will demonstrate the issues and ongoing scholarly debate involved.

First, the general dating of the book is disputed. Many scholars date Deuteronomy to the seventh century B.C. when the Assyrian Empire held sway and the Judean kings Hezekiah and Manasseh reacted, each in his own way, to the crises at hand. Other opinions range from the thirteenth to the fifth century B.C. Second, did Deuteronomy originate in the northern kingdom (perhaps as an internal reform or the reaction of a disenfranchised group) or are its origins in the southern kingdom? Third, as with many biblical books, authorship is another question. Were the authors priests, Levites, prophets, sages, scribes, elders, or a combination of circles with a common agenda? Fourth, there remain issues surrounding redaction toward the canonical text we now have. Many scholars speak roughly of Deuteronomy 5–26, 28 as the core of the book, with the opening and closing chapters as later additions in light of the exile. Others suggest alternative delimitations. Further, there is the account of the high priest Hilkiah finding a scroll of the law in the temple during Josiah's reign (2 Kgs 22–23; cf. 2 Chr 34–35). Whether that account is fact or fiction, there are affinities between Deuteronomy and the Josianic reform, which share numerous parallels. One should also note the connection between the basic Deuteronomic Code (Deut 12–26) and the Book of the Covenant (Exod 20–23). Even a casual reading of these two legal documents finds striking parallels. Law is not univocal in the Scriptures but informed by intertextual analysis. Finally, a comparison of the Ten Commandments in Deuteronomy 5:6-21 and Exodus 20:1-17 offers insights into the development of legal traditions.

Despite differences of opinion regarding these and other issues in the history of tradition, one cannot dismiss the impact of the Babylonian exile on Deuteronomistic history and theology. The Lord God was not responsible for the fall of Israel and then Judah. The people were unfaithful to the vision of the great themes of promise, election, covenant, and law. They were in the grip of a great crisis to which the nations' ancient traditions still offered a message of hope and a challenge to return to the Lord. An example is the story of the monarchy in 1–2 Kings. These books represent a review of a sacred Israelite institution in light of Deuteronomic concerns, particularly the legacy of corrupt kings and emphasis on the centrality of the Jerusalem cult.

In sum, Deuteronomy is about reform and restoration, looking to the past with an eye to the future. Its tone is urgent and appeals to the individual as well as the community. Everyone is called to respond to the Lord's statutes and commandments *today* (4:40).

The literary artistry of Deuteronomy

Deuteronomy picks up where Numbers leaves off. However, these two books have different emphases. Numbers is essentially indirect discourse while Deuteronomy is mostly direct speech. Further, Deuteronomy tends to present a more refined and humane legal spirit. A good example is the distinction of wives from other property in the ninth commandment (5:21). Deuteronomy is not a recounting of past events that no longer impact on life and faith, but a program for the future.

Building on the contributions of the modern historical-critical method, more recent studies have moved to the literary analysis of biblical texts. Such analysis pays close attention to techniques such as repetition, comparison, contrast, irony, wordplay, chiasm, inclusion (also called *inclusio*), and numerical symmetry. The book of Deuteronomy lends itself to such methodologies (rhetorical, narrative, canonical, structural, reader-response, etc.).

Perhaps more than any other Old Testament book Deuteronomy is characterized by repetitive themes and motifs, many of which should be familiar to those who have read the book in its entirety or heard its liturgical proclamation through the years. One thinks of the motif of the land, or the theologies of love, remembering/forgetting, time, and retribution, the Divine Name and the Lord as warrior, the Ten Commandments, the great Shema (Deut 6:4ff), and the enjoining of humane interaction among persons of every class. The Ten Commandments and the great Shema are central to Deuteronomy. Both are relational in nature. The commandments spell out the essentials of a proper relationship between God and others. The Shema complements the Ten Commandments with a counterpoint, i.e., what are the characteristics of this proper relationship? They are love, fidelity, and obedience. Such themes and motifs will be highlighted in the course of this commentary to inform the reader's understanding of the theological message therein. Where notable, attention will also be given to more recent methodologies, including feminist and sociocultural approaches, which have enriched the understanding and appreciation of Deuteronomy. Attention to intertextuality, i.e., interconnections with other biblical texts, will also be noted in course.

In Deuteronomy the reader encounters a grand sermon by Moses on the plains of Moab as the Israelites prepare to cross the Jordan from the east and enter Canaan. This sermon is usually divided into four addresses delimited by editorial superscriptions: "These are the words" (1:1), "This is the law" (4:44), "Moses summoned all Israel" (29:1), and "This is the blessing" (33:1). Each speech has its own emphases while at the same time harking back to what precedes and anticipating what follows. Indeed, "These are the words" is an appropriate beginning and title for Deuteronomy. More than in any other book in the Pentateuch or subsequent historical books words are important in Deuteronomy, words repeated over and over to instruct the people and drill torah into them and future generations (6:7).

It is noteworthy that Deuteronomy characterizes Moses with all the complexity of human nature, including its shadow sides. Moses presents not so much a code of laws (though laws are enjoined) as an impassioned exhortation to live in covenant with the Lord, the one God of Israel. Moses, that reluctant but ever-growing leader in the book of Exodus, has been condemned not to enter the land (32:48-52; cf. Num 20:7-12); he neither becomes bitter nor turns from God but remains an example of unwavering loyalty and service. He obeys the Lord's command to impose hands upon Joshua and commission him as the new leader of journeying Israel. Such steadfastness contrasts with Moses' characterization in the book of Exodus where he doubts his ability (Exod 3:11; 4:1) and argues with the Lord (Exod 5:22-23). Despite his fate Moses is remembered at the end of Deuteronomy as a prophet without equal and an incomparable worker of signs and wonders (34:10-12). Moses' trust in the Lord is praised in later wisdom literature. His memory is held in benediction and God's honor conveyed to him (Sir 45:1-5).

The reader is encouraged to use the commentary with an eye to the Review Aids and Discussion Topics provided at the end. It is also helpful to utilize other biblical resources in studying the rich, complex, and timeless message of Deuteronomy. These resources include other commentaries, concordances, dictionaries, and, of course, the Bible itself.

Outline of the Book of Deuteronomy

Deut 1:1–4:43	Moses' First Address
Deut 4:44–28:69	Moses' Second Address
Deut 29:1–32:52	Moses' Third Address
Deut 33:1–34:12	Moses' Fourth Address

The Book of Deuteronomy

I. First Address

◀ **1** **Introduction.** ¹These are the words that Moses spoke to all Israel beyond the Jordan in the wilderness, in the Arabah, opposite Suph, between Paran and Tophel, Laban, Hazeroth, and Dizahab. ²It is a journey of eleven days from Horeb to Kadesh-barnea by way of the highlands of Seir.

³In the fortieth year, on the first day of the eleventh month, Moses spoke to the Israelites according to all that the Lord had commanded him to speak to them, ⁴after he had defeated Sihon, king of the Amorites, who reigned in Heshbon, and Og, king of Bashan, who reigned in Ashtaroth and in Edrei. ⁵Beyond the Jordan, in the land of Moab, Moses undertook to explain this law:

MOSES' FIRST ADDRESS

Deuteronomy 1:1–4:43

1:1-5 The introduction to Deuteronomy

The Hebrew title for Deuteronomy comes from its opening words, *ʾēlleh haddĕbārîm*, "These are the words . . ." It is from the Greek translation, called the Septuagint, that we get the name Deuteronomy or "second law." As with many biblical books, the opening verses set the stage for what follows. Moses, Israel, and the Lord stand in opposition to the kings and kingdoms of Canaan. The striking geographical details in these few verses call to mind Exodus 14:1-9 where Israel takes its stand against Pharaoh and his army at carefully designated points by the Red Sea. In both scenes the Lord is the guarantor of Israel's security. Further, *all* of Israel is gathered to hear *all* the commands of the Lord through Moses (vv. 1, 3). This is a communal event of grand proportions and with lasting implications. As at the

▶ This symbol indicates a cross reference number in the *Catechism of the Catholic Church*. See page 111 for number citations.

Departure from Horeb. ⁶The LORD, our God, said to us at Horeb: You have stayed long enough at this mountain. ⁷Leave here and go to the hill country of the Amorites and to all the surrounding regions, the Arabah, the mountains, the Shephelah, the Negeb and the seacoast— the land of the Canaanites and the Lebanon as far as the Great River, the Euphrates. ⁸See, I have given that land over to you. Go now and possess the land that the LORD swore to your ancestors, Abraham, Isaac, and Jacob, to give to them and to their descendants after them.

Appointment of Elders. ⁹At that time I said to you, "I am unable to carry you by myself. ¹⁰The LORD, your God, has made you numerous, and now you are as numerous as the stars of the heavens. ¹¹May the LORD, the God of your ancestors, increase you a thousand times over, and bless you as he promised! ¹²But how can I, by myself, bear the weight, the contentiousness of you? ¹³Provide wise, discerning, and reputable persons for each of your tribes, that I may appoint them as your leaders." ¹⁴You answered me, "What you have proposed is good." ¹⁵So I took the leaders of your tribes, wise

---

Red Sea, Israel must take its stand as it prepares to cross the Jordan, and takes a stand against Sihon and Og. Israel's victory over them is reiterated later in Deuteronomy and remembered in tradition (Neh 9:22; Pss 135:10-11; 136:17-22). With this introductory information, Moses commences his extended discourse on torah.

1:6-18 Departure and appointment of elders

The motif of the land is introduced in the context of promise and fulfillment (vv. 7, 8 [2x]). Promise recalls divine commitment in the covenant relationship with the ancestors (Gen 12:1-3; 15:18-21), and fulfillment now demands abiding trust in the Lord. The land bestowed is the Lord's gift to Israel and ideally encompasses a variety of terrain and climates from the Euphrates River in the north to the Negeb (reclaimed desert) in the south. The land motif is important in Deuteronomy because it recalls that the landless people journeyed in trust of the promise of a fertile land, a memory that stirs (in readers and hearers of the book) thoughts both of the exodus and the return from Babylonian exile in Israelite later history and theology. Further, the land is intimately connected to observance of the law (5:31; 12:1). The land could be lost, as Israel found out in the course of time. In sum, going forth under divine promise, trust on the journey, and observance of divine commands in the land are intrinsically related.

The selection of elders in 1:9-18 may seem to interrupt the flow of the narrative. However, this episode anticipates the important theme of leader-

and reputable, and set them as leaders over you, commanders over thousands, over hundreds, over fifties and over tens, and other tribal officers. ¹⁶I charged your judges at that time, "Listen to complaints among your relatives, and administer true justice to both parties even if one of them is a resident alien. ¹⁷In rendering judgment, do not consider who a person is; give ear to the lowly and to the great alike, fearing no one, for the judgment is God's. Any case that is too difficult for you bring to me and I will hear it." ¹⁸Thus I charged you, at that time, with all the things you were to do.

The Twelve Scouts. ¹⁹Then we set out from Horeb and journeyed through that whole vast and fearful wilderness that you have seen, in the direction of

ship in Deuteronomy (e.g., judges, priests, and prophets in 17:8–18:22) and culminates in Joshua's marching before the people under the protection of the Lord (31:1-6). Shared leadership by elders and other persons is a response to increase in numbers among the Israelites (an aspect of blessing) and the people's occasional murmuring (an important and widespread motif in the Old Testament). Increase harks back to the book of Exodus where Pharaoh reacts with oppression to counter the prolific growth of his Hebrew slaves (Exod 1:7-10; cf. Gen 1:28).

The star motif (v. 10; 10:22) highlights fertility, a reference back to the promise of descendants to Abraham (Gen 15:5; 22:17; 26:4), and anticipates in Deuteronomy the warning against the worship of celestial bodies (4:19; cf. Gen 1:16). Further, this motif underscores that for Israel God's throne is set above the stars and celestial bodies. These objects are under divine control (Job 22:12; Ps 147:4; Sir 43:9-10).

The motif of the resident alien (Hebrew *gēr*) emerges in verse 16. Together with the widow and orphan, this triad of vulnerable and often exploited persons enjoys special protection in Deuteronomic theology. In sum, this opening section affirms the perennial value of collaborative leadership and equal justice under the law. Israel must be careful to keep all the laws cited in the course of Moses' grand speech, because judgment belongs to God (v. 17).

1:19-46 The debacle at Kadesh-barnea

The land is a promised gift, but at the same time it must be taken by force. Will the Israelites trust that the Lord is present with them as they march forth? This tension recalls the Israelites' fear at the Red Sea, which is later juxtaposed with their breaking into joyful song (Exod 14:10-14;

the hill country of the Amorites, as the LORD, our God, had commanded; and we came to Kadesh-barnea. ²⁰I said to you, "You have come to the hill country of the Amorites, which the LORD, our God, is giving us. ²¹See, the LORD, your God, has given this land over to you. Go up and take possession of it, as the LORD, the God of your ancestors, has promised you. Do not fear or be dismayed." ²²Then all of you approached me and said, "Let us send men ahead to spy out the land for us and report to us on the road we should follow and the cities we will come upon." ²³Agreeing with the proposal, I took twelve men from your number, one from each tribe. ²⁴They set out into the hill country as far as the Wadi Eshcol, and explored it. ²⁵Then, taking along some of the fruit of the land, they brought it down to us and reported, "The land the LORD, our God, is giving us is good."

Threats of Revolt. ²⁶But you refused to go up; you defied the command of the LORD, your God. ²⁷You set to murmuring in your tents, "Out of hatred for us the LORD has brought us out of the land of Egypt, to deliver us into the power of the Amorites and destroy us. ²⁸What shall we meet with up there? Our men have made our hearts melt by saying, 'The people are bigger and taller than we, and their cities are large and fortified to the sky; besides, we saw the Anakim there.'"

²⁹But I said to you, "Have no dread or fear of them. ³⁰The LORD, your God, who goes before you, is the one who will fight for you, just as he acted with you before your very eyes in Egypt, ³¹as well as in the wilderness, where you saw how the LORD, your God, carried you, as one carries his own child, all along your journey until you arrived at this place." ³²Despite

---

15:1-3). The psalms extol the Lord as warrior (Pss 68:1-4; 114:1-8; 124:1-8) despite numerous military defeats recounted in Israel's history. The book of Deuteronomy concludes with an affirmation of security under the Lord (32:10-14).

At this juncture the tension between security and fear is dramatized via engagement between the Israelites and the indigenous peoples. Israelite scouts reconnoiter the land and bring back an encouraging report, including some token fruit from the land. This good news is met with murmuring and fear. The Israelites must face the great and tall indigenous peoples, including the Amorites and the Anakim. The Anakim (9:1-2; cf. Num 13:30-33) are eventually conquered by Joshua and take refuge in Philistine cities (Josh 11:21-22). Such references to the enemy are probably more symbolic than references to real geography and history. They represent the arousal of fear and certainty of defeat against the enemy, calling to mind the David and Goliath story (1 Sam 17) and other such narratives.

this, you would not trust the LORD, your God, ³³who journeys before you to find you a place to camp—by night in the fire, and by day in the cloud, to show you the way to go. ³⁴When the LORD heard your words, he was angry, and took an oath: ³⁵Not a single one of this evil generation shall look upon the good land I swore to give to your ancestors, ³⁶except Caleb, son of Jephunneh. He shall see it, for to him and to his descendants I will give the land he trod upon, because he has fully followed the LORD.

³⁷The LORD was angered against me also on your account, and said, You shall not enter there either, ³⁸but Joshua, son of Nun, your attendant, shall enter. Encourage him, for he is the one who is to give Israel its possession. ³⁹Your little ones, who you said would become plunder, and your children, who as yet do not know good from evil—they shall enter there; to them I will give it, and they shall take possession of it. ⁴⁰But as for yourselves: turn back and proceed into the wilderness on the Red Sea road.

Unsuccessful Invasion. ⁴¹In reply you said to me, "We have sinned against the LORD. We will go up ourselves and fight, just as the LORD, our God, commanded us." And each of you girded on his weapons, making light of going up into the hill country. ⁴²But the LORD said to me, Warn them: Do not go up and fight—for I will not be in your midst—lest you be beaten down before your enemies. ⁴³I gave you this warning but you would not listen. You defied the LORD's command and arrogantly went off into the hill country. ⁴⁴Then the Amorites living in that hill country came out against you and put you to flight the way bees do, cutting you down in Seir as far as Hormah. ⁴⁵On your return you wept before the LORD, but the LORD did not listen to your voice or give ear to you. ⁴⁶That is why you had to stay as long as you did at Kadesh.

In addition to fear, seeing is another theme. The Israelites already saw a fearful desert but safely crossed it (v. 19). Will they remember what they saw and see it happening now as the Lord carries them along (vv. 30-31)? Will they let the sight of threatening opponents compromise their trust in the Lord?

Fear and disobedience overwhelm trust and confidence at this juncture. Longing for the past overshadows their envisioning of a bright and promising future in the land (v. 25). It is noteworthy that their failure to trust (v. 32) is expressed by the Hebrew active participle. This verbal subtlety highlights the ongoing and pervasive nature of their distrust and unbelief. The tentative and unsuccessful first scouting of the land leaves the Israelites sojourned for a long time at Kadesh-barnea.

2 Northward Along Edom.

¹Then we turned and proceeded into the wilderness on the Red Sea road, as the LORD had told me, and circled around the highlands of Seir for a long time. ²Finally the LORD said to me, ³You have wandered round these highlands long enough; turn and go north. ⁴Command the people: You are now about to pass through the territory of your relatives, the descendants of Esau, who live in Seir. Though they are afraid of you, be very careful ⁵not to come in conflict with them, for I will not give you so much as a foot of their land, since I have already given Esau possession of the highlands of Seir. ⁶You shall purchase from them with money the food you eat; even the water you drink you shall buy from them with money. ⁷Surely, the LORD, your God, has blessed you in all your undertakings; he has been concerned about your journey through this vast wilderness. It is now forty years that the LORD, your God, has been with you, and you have lacked nothing. ⁸So we passed by our relatives, the descendants of Esau who live in Seir, leaving behind us the Arabah route, Elath, and Ezion-geber.

Along Moab. Then we turned and passed on toward the wilderness of Moab. ⁹And the LORD said to me, Do not show hostility to the Moabites or engage them in battle, for I will not give you possession of any of their land, since I have given Ar to the descendants of Lot as their possession. ¹⁰(Formerly the Emim lived there, a people great and numerous and as tall as the Anakim; ¹¹like the Anakim they are considered Rephaim, though the Moabites call them Emim. ¹²In Seir, however, the former inhabitants were the Horites; the descendants of Esau dispossessed them, clearing them out of the way and dwelling in their place, just as Israel has done in the land of its possession which the LORD gave it.) ¹³Now get ready to cross the Wadi Zered.

So we crossed the Wadi Zered. ¹⁴Now thirty-eight years had elapsed between our departure from Kadesh-barnea and the crossing of the Wadi Zered; in the meantime the whole generation of soldiers had perished from the camp, as the LORD had sworn they should. ¹⁵Indeed the LORD's own hand was against them, to rout them from the camp completely.

Along Ammon. ¹⁶When at length death had put an end to all the soldiers among the people, ¹⁷the LORD said to me, ¹⁸You are now about to leave Ar and the territory of Moab behind. ¹⁹As you come

---

2:1–3:11 From Edom to Bashan

Edom, Moab, and Ammon permit easy transit for the wandering Israelites in Transjordan, while the Amorites and Bashan resist and engage in battle. The Deuteronomic tradition differs to some degree from similar accounts in Numbers 20–21 and 33:37-49. For example, in Numbers the Israelites must circumvent a hostile Edom, and the land is specifically referred to as Edom rather than the descendants of Esau (Num 21:4; cf. Gen 25:21-26).

opposite the Ammonites, do not show hostility or come in conflict with them, for I will not give you possession of any land of the Ammonites, since I have given it to the descendants of Lot as their possession. ²⁰(This also is considered a country of the Rephaim; formerly the Rephaim dwelt there. The Ammonites call them Zamzummim, ²¹a people great and numerous and as tall as the Anakim. But these, too, the LORD cleared out of the way for the Ammonites, so that they dispossessed them and dwelt in their place. ²²He did the same for the descendants of Esau, who live in Seir, by clearing the Horites out of their way, so that they dispossessed them and dwelt in their place down to the present. ²³As for the Avvim, who once lived in villages in the vicinity of Gaza, the Caphtorim, migrating from Caphtor, cleared them away and dwelt in their place.)

Defeat of Sihon. ²⁴Advance now across the Wadi Arnon. I now deliver into your power Sihon, the Amorite king of Heshbon, and his land. Begin to take possession; engage him in battle. ²⁵This day I will begin to put a fear and dread of you into the peoples everywhere under heaven, so that at the mention of your name they will quake and tremble before you.

²⁶So I sent messengers from the wilderness of Kedemoth to Sihon, king of Heshbon, with this offer of peace: ²⁷"Let me pass through your country. I will travel only on the road. I will not turn aside either to the right or to the left. ²⁸The food I eat you will sell me for money, and the water I drink, you will give me for money. Only let me march through, ²⁹as the descendants of Esau who dwell in Seir and the Moabites who dwell in Ar have done, until I cross the Jordan into the land the LORD, our God, is about to give us." ³⁰But Sihon, king of Heshbon, refused to let us pass through his land, because the LORD, your God, made him stubborn in mind and obstinate in heart that he might deliver him into your power, as indeed he has now done.

³¹Then the LORD said to me, Now that I have already begun to give over to you Sihon and his land, begin to take possession. ³²So Sihon and all his people advanced against us to join battle at Jahaz; ³³but since the LORD, our God, had given him over to us, we defeated him and his sons and all his people. ³⁴At that time we captured all his cities and put every city under the ban, men, women and children; we left no survivor. ³⁵Our only plunder was the livestock and the spoils of the

---

The narrative moves from a description of peaceful passage to warfare, with the Lord in control of Israel's movement at every turn. During their crossing through Edom, Moab, and Ammon, the Israelites are ordered not to fight because the Lord has given these lands to other peoples from among the wider family of Abraham (2:5, 9, 19). In warfare against the Amorites and Bashan, the Israelites are assured victory through divine intervention, including the Lord's hardening of Sihon's heart (2:30; cf. Exod 4:21; 8:15

captured cities. ³⁶From Aroer on the edge of the Wadi Arnon and from the town in the wadi itself, as far as Gilead, no city was too well fortified for us. All of them the LORD, our God, gave over to us. ³⁷However, just as the LORD, our God, commanded us, you did not encroach upon any of the Ammonite land, neither the region bordering on the Wadi Jabbok, nor the cities of the highlands.

3 Defeat of Og. ¹Then we turned and proceeded up the road to Bashan. But Og, king of Bashan, came out against us with all his people to give battle at Edrei. ²The LORD said to me, Do not be afraid of him, for I have delivered him into your power with all his people and his land. Do to him as you did to Sihon, king of the Amorites, who reigned in Heshbon. ³And thus the LORD, our God, delivered into our power also Og, king of Bashan, with all his people. We defeated him so completely that we left him no survivor. ⁴At that time we captured all his cities; there was no town we did not take: sixty cities in all, the whole region of Argob, the kingdom of Og in Bashan—⁵all these cities were fortified with high walls and gates and bars—besides a great number of unwalled towns. ⁶As we had done to Sihon, king of Heshbon, so also here we put all the

on Pharaoh). Ironically, the Israelites who so recently were fearful of the indigenous people are now feared themselves (2:4, 25).

It is noteworthy that the lands not given over to the Israelites are identified with their own kin, Esau and Lot. Esau's hairiness (Gen 25:25) is related by folk etymology to the name of the region of Seir where he eventually settles. Ancient Seir (meaning "hairy") was situated along a rugged, thickly forested mountain range, the appearance of which gave rise to the association with hairiness. Lot is the great ancestor of the Ammonites and Moabites (Gen 19:30-38). The lands given over to the Israelites are bestowed on the tribes of Reuben and Gad, as well as two clans of Manasseh. Whether by entitlement or bestowal, the new land is linked to kinship among the tribes. Deuteronomic theology highlights the fact that the Lord's gift of land is more than violent conquest and that blood ties have an abiding value. Relationships engage people with God and with one another despite conflict and mutual claims to the same territory. The Lord is not solely the God of Israel but also of the nations. Gratitude for divine favor must not be exclusive but celebrated with and for others.

The ecological destruction and human genocide against the Amorites and Bashan may strike the modern reader as extreme and morally distasteful (2:34; 3:6-7). Only spoils of livestock and loot, not human persons, are of value to the conqueror. However, war is inherently a violent enterprise

towns under the ban, men, women and children; [7]but all the livestock and the spoils of each city we took as plunder for ourselves.

[8]And so at that time we took from the two kings of the Amorites beyond the Jordan the territory from the Wadi Arnon to Mount Hermon [9](the Sidonians call Hermon Sirion and the Amorites call it Senir), [10]all the towns of the plateau, all of Gilead, and all of Bashan as far as Salecah and Edrei, towns of the kingdom of Og in Bashan. [11](Og, king of Bashan, was the last remaining survivor of the Rephaim. He had a bed of iron, nine regular cubits long and four wide, which

is still preserved in Rabbah of the Ammonites.)

Allotment of the Conquered Lands. [12]As for the land we took possession of at that time, I gave Reuben and Gad the territory from Aroer, on the edge of the Wadi Arnon, halfway up into the highlands of Gilead, with its cities. [13]The rest of Gilead and all of Bashan, the kingdom of Og, I gave to the half-tribe of Manasseh. (The whole Argob region, all that part of Bashan, was once called a land of the Rephaim. [14]Jair, a Manassite, took all the region of Argob as far as the border of the Geshurites and Maacathites, and named them—Bashan, that is—after

and says more about human nature and desire than divine will. Decimation of the enemy is more about military strategy and taking spoils than moral values (20:10-20). Nations tend to presume that God goes forth with *their* armies. So-called Holy War (perhaps better "Wars of Yнwн" or "Wars of the Lord") and the theology of warfare are more reflective of perceived ideals than of historical fact. Any claims, territorial or otherwise, are not solely the result of human prowess but the will of God at work in the created order. Theologically, the narrative highlights the tension between divine freedom and the vagaries of human freedom.

3:12-29 Allotment of the land and plight of Moses

The first apportionment of land to certain tribes of Israel is more than simply a geographical division. Taking possession of the land is the result of a struggle that includes conflict and loss of life on the battlefield. However, the land is ultimately a gift and the fulfillment of divine promises. This gift stems from divine love of Israel (7:6) and judgment on the wicked indigenous nations (9:5).

This first gift of land leads to the first prayer of Moses in Deuteronomy (vv. 24-25). He begs to touch the land beyond the Jordan, only to be rebuffed by God. The priestly tradition (P) offers an explanation, i.e., Moses' breaking faith at the waters of Meribah (32:51-52; cf. Num 20:12), but in

himself, Havvoth-jair, the name it bears today.) ¹⁵To Machir I gave Gilead, ¹⁶and to Reuben and Gad the territory from Gilead to the Wadi Arnon—the middle of the wadi being its boundary—and to the Wadi Jabbok, which is the border of the Ammonites, ¹⁷as well as the Arabah with the Jordan and its banks from Chinnereth to the Salt Sea of the Arabah, under the slopes of Pisgah on the east.

¹⁸At that time I charged you: The Lord, your God, has given you this land as your possession. But all your troops equipped for battle must cross over in the vanguard of your fellow Israelites. ¹⁹But your wives and children, as well as your livestock, of which I know you have a large number, shall remain behind in the towns I have given you, ²⁰until the Lord has settled your relatives as well, and they too possess the land which the Lord, your God, will give them on the other side of the Jordan. Then you may all return to the possessions I have given you.

²¹And I charged Joshua as well, "Your own eyes have seen all that the Lord, your God, has done to both these kings; so, too, will the Lord do to all the kingdoms into which you will cross over. ²²Do not fear them, for it is the Lord, your God, who will fight for you."

Moses Excluded from the Promised Land. ²³It was then that I entreated the Lord, ²⁴"Lord God, you have begun to show to your servant your greatness and your mighty hand. What god in heaven or on earth can perform deeds and powerful acts like yours? ²⁵Ah, let me cross over and see the good land beyond the Jordan, that fine hill country, and the Lebanon!" ²⁶But the Lord was angry with me on your account and would not hear me. The Lord said to me, Enough! Speak to me no more of this. ²⁷Go up to the top of Pisgah and look out to the west, and to the north, and to the south, and to the east. Look well, for you shall not cross this Jordan. ²⁸Commission Joshua, and encourage and strengthen him, for it is he who will cross at the head of this people and he who will give them possession of the land you are to see.

²⁹So we remained in the valley opposite Beth-peor.

Deuteronomy the explanation is mitigated in line with Deuteronomic theology. Here Moses takes on a punitive judgment for the sake of the people, a hint of the scriptural theme of vicarious suffering of one for the many (Isa 53:4-6). Moses is barred from the land on their account, a detail repeated in the narrative to emphasize the point (1:37; 3:26; 4:21), but Moses is not passive; he makes an appeal (vv. 23-25; cf. Gen 18:22-33 on Abraham).

One more time Moses climbs a mountain. Pisgah is a mountain in northwestern Moab and close to Mount Nebo, the mountain on which, according to tradition, Moses died and was buried. Pisgah is also the site where Balak built seven altars and Balaam spoke oracles over Israel (Num 23:14-26).

4 **Advantages of Fidelity.** [1]Now therefore, Israel, hear the statutes and ordinances I am teaching you to observe, that you may live, and may enter in and take possession of the land which the LORD, the God of your ancestors, is giving you. [2]In your observance of the commandments of the LORD, your God, which I am commanding you, you shall not add to what I command you nor subtract from it. [3]You have seen with your own eyes what the LORD did at Baal-peor: the LORD, your God, destroyed from your midst everyone who followed the Baal of Peor; [4]but you, who held fast to the LORD, your God, are all alive today. [5]See, I am teaching you the statutes and ordinances as the LORD, my God, has commanded me, that you may observe them in the land you are entering to possess. [6]Observe them carefully, for this is your wisdom and discernment in the sight of the peoples, who will hear of all these statutes and say, "This great nation is truly a wise and discerning people." [7]For what great nation is there that has gods so close to it as the LORD, our God, is to us whenever we call upon him? [8]Or what great nation has statutes and ordinances that are as just as this whole law which I am setting before you today?

4:1-40 The call to fidelity

The first discourse of Moses concludes with a reminder of what God has done for the Israelites and what they in turn must observe. Observance is concretized and lived out by means of statutes, ordinances, decrees, and commands. This exhortation is highlighted by an inclusion, i.e., repetition of a word or phrase at the beginning and end of a unit (vv. 1, 40), where the theme of statutes given by the Lord for long life is repeated. "Life" is a word that echoes throughout Deuteronomy (4:1; 5:29, 33; 6:24; 30:19-20; 32:43).

Various themes and motifs run through the speech. First, the people are directed toward observance. The Hebrew verb for "observance" denotes having charge over, tending, and keeping watch like a sentinel. Such vigilance characterizes observance of the commandments. Second, teaching children is emphasized throughout. Instruction must be passed down to subsequent generations (6:7). This mandate both harks back to the Passover ritual question: "What does this rite of yours mean?" (Exod 10:2; 12:24-27) and anticipates the pedagogy of wisdom literature (Prov 1:8; Sir 2:1-6). Third, the sevenfold repetition of "fire" punctuates the recounting of the theophany at Horeb (vv. 11, 12, 15, 24, 33, 36 [2x]). Fire both illumines and consumes, a fitting metaphor for the divine presence and activity in the created order. The reference to consuming fire in verse 24 (the very center

Revelation at Horeb. ⁹However, be on your guard and be very careful not to forget the things your own eyes have seen, nor let them slip from your heart as long as you live, but make them known to your children and to your children's children, ¹⁰that day you stood before the LORD, your God, at Horeb, when the LORD said to me: Assemble the people for me, that I may let them hear my words, that they may learn to fear me as long as they live in the land and may so teach their children. ¹¹You came near and stood at the foot of the mountain, while the mountain blazed to the heart of the heavens with fire and was enveloped in a dense black cloud. ¹²Then the LORD spoke to you from the midst of the fire. You heard the sound of the words, but saw no form; there was only a voice. ¹³He proclaimed to you his covenant, which he commanded you to keep: the ten words, which he wrote on two stone tablets. ¹⁴At that time the LORD charged me to teach you the statutes and ordinances for you to observe in the land you are about to cross into and possess.

Danger of Idolatry. ¹⁵Because you saw no form at all on the day the LORD spoke to you at Horeb from the midst of the fire, be strictly on your guard ¹⁶not to act corruptly by fashioning an idol for yourselves to represent any figure, whether it be the form of a man or of a woman, ¹⁷the form of any animal on the earth, the form of any bird that flies in the sky, ¹⁸the form of anything that crawls on the ground, or the form of any fish in the waters under the earth. ¹⁹And when you look up to the heavens and behold the sun or the moon or the stars, the whole heavenly host, do not be led astray into bowing down to them and serving them. These the LORD, your God, has apportioned to all the other nations under the heavens; ²⁰but you the LORD has taken and led out of that iron foundry, Egypt, that you might be his people, his heritage, as you are today. ²¹But the LORD was angry with me on your account and swore that I should not cross the Jordan nor enter the good land which the LORD, your God, is giving you as a heritage. ²²I myself shall die in this country; I shall not cross the Jordan; but you are going to cross over and take possession of that good land. ²³Be careful, therefore, lest you forget the covenant which the LORD, your God, has made with you, and fashion for yourselves against his command an idol in any form whatsoever. ²⁴For the LORD, your God, is a consuming fire, a jealous God.

God's Fidelity and Love. ²⁵When you have children and children's children, and have grown old in the land, should

---

of the fire motif here) links fire to divine jealousy. The Hebrew word for jealousy means fiery red, a fitting image. Fire remains today a liturgical appointment in many Christian liturgical settings, including the Easter candle, altar candles, and the sanctuary lamp.

The dangers of idolatry are also noted. The phrase "You heard the sound of the words, but saw no form . . ." (vv. 12, 15) emphasizes divine tran-

you then act corruptly by fashioning an idol in the form of anything, and by this evil done in his sight provoke the LORD, your God, ²⁶I call heaven and earth this day to witness against you, that you shall all quickly perish from the land which you are crossing the Jordan to possess. You shall not live in it for any length of time but shall be utterly wiped out. ²⁷The LORD will scatter you among the peoples, and there shall remain but a handful of you among the nations to which the LORD will drive you. ²⁸There you shall serve gods that are works of human hands, of wood and stone, gods which can neither see nor hear, neither eat nor smell. ²⁹Yet when you seek the LORD, your God, from there, you shall indeed find him if you search after him with all your heart and soul. ³⁰In your distress, when all these things shall have come upon you, you shall finally return to the LORD, your God, and listen to his voice. ³¹Since the LORD, your God, is a merciful God, he will not abandon or destroy you, nor forget the covenant with your ancestors that he swore to them.

³²Ask now of the days of old, before your time, ever since God created humankind upon the earth; ask from one end of the sky to the other: Did anything so great ever happen before? Was it ever heard of? ³³Did a people ever hear the voice of God speaking from the midst of fire, as you did, and live? ³⁴Or did any god venture to go and take a nation for himself from the midst of another nation, by testings, by signs and wonders, by war, with strong hand and out-stretched arm, and by great terrors, all of which the LORD, your God, did for you in Egypt before your very eyes? ³⁵All this you were allowed to see that you might know that the LORD is God; there is no other. ³⁶Out of the heavens he let you hear his voice to discipline you; on earth he let you see his great fire, and you heard him speaking out of the fire. ³⁷For love of your ancestors he chose their descendants after them and by his presence and great power led you out of Egypt, ³⁸dispossessing before you nations greater and mightier than you, so as to bring you in and to give their land to you as a heritage, as it is today. ³⁹This is why you must now acknowledge, and fix in your heart, that the LORD is God in the heavens above and on earth below, and that there is no other. ⁴⁰And you must keep his statutes and commandments which I command you today, that you and your children after you may prosper, and that you may have long life on the land which the LORD, your God, is giving you forever.

---

scendence and the futility of incantations and the use of similar practices to manipulate God. Such conduct is not in compliance with the Ten Commandments (5:7-8). Idols, objects of false worship, can either be the powerful, observable forces of nature that impact life and the cycle of seasons (sun, moon, and stars) or works of human hands that tell more about human need than divine attributes.

Cities of Refuge. ⁴¹Then Moses set apart three cities in the region east of the Jordan, ⁴²to which a homicide might flee who killed a neighbor unintentionally, where there had been no hatred previously, so that the killer might flee to one of these cities and live: ⁴³Bezer in the wilderness, in the region of the plateau, for the Reubenites; Ramoth in Gilead for the Gadites; and Golan in Bashan for the Manassites.

II. Second Address

A. The Lord's Covenant with Israel

Introduction. ⁴⁴This is the law which Moses set before the Israelites. ⁴⁵These are the decrees, and the statutes and ordi-

---

Finally, the speech introduces another important theme in Deuteronomy, i.e., the grand theology of remembering/forgetting (v. 23; see 5:15; 7:18; 8:2, 18-19, etc.). The faithful must remember the covenant with the Lord, a value closely connected to teaching children. Not to remember and not to teach suppress the great saga of the people, a lesson reprised in the wisdom literature (Sir 28:6-7).

4:41-43 Cities of refuge

Mosaic law provides places of asylum to those who kill without malice. This institution is unique to Israel in the Scriptures. The topic is added on here and discussed in more detail later (19:1-13; cf. Num 35:9-15 where six cities are provided to harbor the refugee from blood vengeance). Joshua 20 calls for a trial and actually names the six cities. The book of Numbers focuses on harboring the culprit in a limited area until he makes an appearance before the community. Since clan vengeance would pollute the land, Deuteronomy emphasizes the protection of the innocent blood of accidental death from such clan vengeance. The caring spirit of Deuteronomy comes through on this issue. The Lord is the source of justice, and human life is sacred. Vigilante justice must never be allowed to gain the upper hand.

MOSES' SECOND ADDRESS

Deuteronomy 4:44–28:69

4:44-49 Introduction

These verses are similar to the introduction to the first address (1:1-5) in that they cite precise geographical locations. From this point in the narrative, references to statutes, ordinances, decrees, and similar terms become more common. The address dovetails into the Ten Commandments and the great Shema, followed by various laws sanctioned by curses and blessings.

Map of Canaan

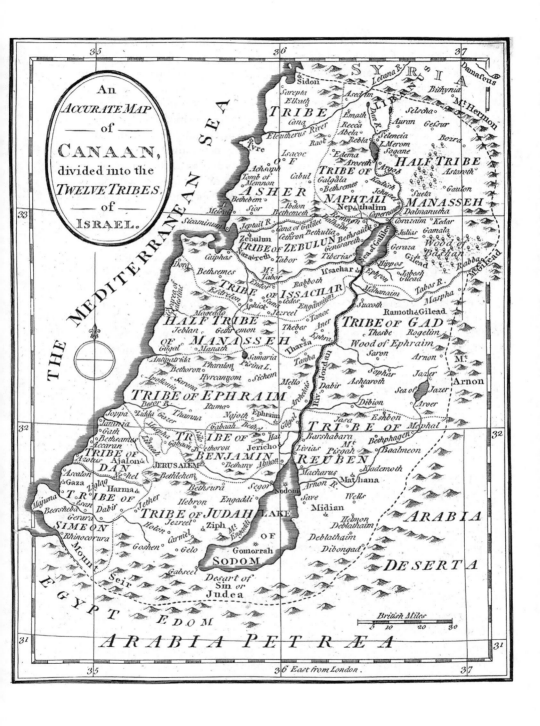

nances which Moses proclaimed to the Israelites after they came out of Egypt, ⁴⁶beyond the Jordan in the valley opposite Beth-peor, in the land of Sihon, king of the Amorites, who reigned in Heshbon, whom Moses and the Israelites defeated after they came out of Egypt. ⁴⁷They took possession of his land and the land of Og, king of Bashan, as well—the land of these two kings of the Amorites in the region beyond the Jordan to the east: ⁴⁸from Aroer on the edge of the Wadi Arnon to Mount Sion (that is, Hermon) ⁴⁹and all the Arabah beyond Jordan to the east, as far as the Arabah Sea under the slopes of Pisgah.

5 **The Covenant at Horeb.** ¹Moses summoned all Israel and said to them, Hear, O Israel, the statutes and ordinances which I proclaim in your hearing this day, that you may learn them and take care to observe them. ²The Lord, our God, made a covenant with us at Horeb; ³not with our ancestors did the Lord make this covenant, but with us, all of us who are alive here this day.

⁴Face to face, the Lord spoke with you ▶ on the mountain from the midst of the fire, ⁵while I was standing between the Lord and you at that time, to announce to you these words of the Lord, since you were afraid of the fire and would not go up the mountain:

The Decalogue. ⁶I am the Lord your ▶ God, who brought you out of the land of Egypt, out of the house of slavery. ⁷You shall not have other gods beside me. ⁸You shall not make for yourself an idol or a likeness of anything in the heavens above or on the earth below or in the waters beneath the earth; ⁹you shall not bow down before them or serve them. For I, the Lord, your God, am a jealous God, bringing punishment for their parents' wickedness on the children of those who hate me, down to the third and fourth generation, ¹⁰but showing love down to the thousandth generation of those who love me and keep my commandments.

¹¹You shall not invoke the name of ▶ the Lord, your God, in vain. For the

---

5:1–6:3 The Ten Commandments

All Israel is summoned to hear the statutes and decrees that stem from covenant with the Lord. The call to "hear" (v. 1) implicitly includes response and obedience, as well as anticipates the great Shema (6:4). The Mosaic covenant is characterized by human obligations, in contrast to the Abrahamic covenant that emphasizes what the Lord will do for Israel (Gen 12:1-4; 15:1-6). Both aspects of covenant complement one another, i.e., the gift of the land fulfills God's promises to the ancestors and in turn demands obedience from the people. The land is not an outright gift with guaranteed security. Further, 5:1-5 shows that Moses speaks to the present and to future generations, and is not simply reciting a nostalgic recollection of past events that have no further impact.

LORD will not leave unpunished anyone who invokes his name in vain.

◄ ¹²Observe the sabbath day—keep it holy, as the LORD, your God, commanded you. ¹³Six days you may labor and do all your work, ¹⁴but the seventh day is a sabbath of the LORD your God. You shall not do any work, either you, your son or your daughter, your male or female slave, your ox or donkey or any work animal, or the resident alien within your gates, so that your male and female slave ◄ may rest as you do. ¹⁵Remember that you too were once slaves in the land of Egypt, and the LORD, your God, brought you out from there with a strong hand and outstretched arm. That is why the LORD, your God, has commanded you to observe the sabbath day.

¹⁶Honor your father and your mother, ► as the LORD, your God, has commanded you, that you may have a long life and that you may prosper in the land the LORD your God is giving you.

¹⁷You shall not kill. ►

¹⁸You shall not commit adultery.

¹⁹You shall not steal. ►

²⁰You shall not bear dishonest witness against your neighbor.

²¹You shall not covet your neighbor's ► wife.

This background sets the stage for the revelation of the Ten Commandments (cf. Exod 20:1-17; the sequence here follows the Catholic and Lutheran division. Other traditions divide the material differently). In both Exodus and Deuteronomy the commandments are offered in the context of a covenant relationship. Further, the Ten Commandments are a monumental revelation mediated and communicated by Moses (5:5). His mediation characterizes other climactic moments in the saga of Israel, such as in Pharaoh's court (Exod 5:1), at the Sea of Reeds (Exod 14:10-16), and the revolt at Kadesh (Num 14:1-25). Despite starting out as a reluctant leader, Moses is remembered as the Lord's preeminent envoy.

The Ten Commandments are not burdensome decrees but an invitation to a relationship characterized by mutual freedom. The God of Israel is free of coercion by magic; the Israelites are free of the burdens of polytheism. The prologue offers an ageless reason for fidelity to these commandments, namely, the Lord freed the people from slavery in Egypt (v. 6).

The first commandment (vv. 7-10) is essentially a demand that Israel have no other gods besides the Lord, a mandate that would often be compromised in the course of Israelite history. This commandment relates both to human and divine freedom. Having no other gods frees the Israelites from the burden of placating a pantheon of gods. The prohibition of carved images preserves the Lord from the superstitious controls of magic and

You shall not desire your neighbor's house or field, his male or female slave, his ox or donkey, or anything that belongs to your neighbor.

◄ **Moses as Mediator.** [22]These words the LORD spoke with a loud voice to your entire assembly on the mountain from the midst of the fire and the dense black cloud, and added no more. He inscribed them on two stone tablets and gave them to me. [23]But when you heard the voice from the midst of the darkness, while the mountain was ablaze with fire, you came near to me, all your tribal heads and elders, [24]and said, "The LORD, our God, has indeed let us see his glory and his greatness, and we have heard his voice from the midst of the fire. Today we have found out that God may speak to a mortal and that person may still live. [25]Now, why should we die? For this great fire will consume us. If we hear the voice of the LORD, our God, any more, we shall die. [26]For what mortal has heard

idol worship. The meaning and practice of authentic religion are in mind here; salvation history spans the promises to the ancestors, the exodus and wilderness experience, the covenant and other key events. Freedom in the land demands total fidelity to the Lord.

The second commandment (v. 11) relates to the first. It preserves the Lord from superstitious control through the use of the divine name. In the ancient world to bestow a name, know a name, or change another's name implied certain authority over the individual. Hence, Adam names the animals and gains stewardship over creation (Gen 2:19-22; cf. 1:28); the Lord designates Abram/Abraham as father of the nations (Gen 17:3-8); and the Lord reveals the divine name YHWH to Moses because an unnamed god is an unknown god in Semitic thought (Exod 3:13-15).

The third commandment (vv. 12-15) regarding the sabbath associates holiness with relaxation from work. To be holy means to be set apart, so the sabbath is set apart as a special day. Sabbath preserves the Israelites from constant labor by providing a day of rest. The spirit of this commandment is reiterated in Deuteronomy 15 where release from debt is discussed. The sabbath is essentially a gift of rest from habitual toil. The ancient world lived under the demand of daily toil in order to eke out a living and the possibility of rest was more an ideal than a reality, given the daily demands of ancient pastoral and agricultural life. The sabbath ideal is found in the prophets as well (Isa 66:22-23) and anticipates the vision of apocalyptic hope of a world with no toil, pain, or death (Rev 21:1-4).

The fourth commandment (v. 16) is a hinge amid the commandments as they move from divine/human relationship to relationships between

the voice of the living God speaking from the midst of fire, as we have, and lived? ²⁷You go closer and listen to all that the LORD, our God, will say, and then tell us what the LORD, our God, tells you; we will listen and obey."

²⁸The LORD heard your words as you were speaking to me and said to me, I have heard the words these people have spoken to you, which are all well said. ²⁹Would that they might always be of such a mind, to fear me and to keep all my commandments! Then they and their descendants would prosper forever. ³⁰Go, tell them: Return to your tents. ³¹Then you stand here near me and I will

---

people. Its original wording may have paralleled the other apodictic commandments here and may have appeared as something like "You shall *not* curse your father and your mother." This commandment preserves the dignity of family life, especially that of the aged when they lose productivity and become burdensome. Old Testament wisdom literature echoes this value (Prov 19:26; 30:17; Sir 3:16; cf. Eph 6:1-3). Hence, this law relates more to the adult children of the sick or elderly than to youths. It is noteworthy that this commandment has a promise attached, i.e., long life in the land. Promises fulfilled permeate Deuteronomy and are associated with reciprocal obedience (4:40; 5:33; 6:2).

The fifth commandment (v. 17) prohibits killing as an individual prerogative apart from divine law and judicial process. The commandment is more related to preserving Israelite life than a universal regard for life in general (Lev 19:17-18; cf. Matt 5:21-22; Luke 10:29-37).

The sixth commandment (v. 18) against adultery preserves the sanctity of marriage and family. The patriarchal society of the ancient world had different standards for men and women. A man committed adultery with a married woman (i.e., against another man's marriage); a woman committed adultery with any man. By most modern standards this seems biased, but the commandment is intended to protect the paternity of offspring and the innate sanctity and exclusivity of marriage.

The seventh commandment against stealing (v. 19) deals more with human persons than property, but the issue of property theft is included in Israelite law as well (Exod 22:1-3, 11). Stealing in this sense includes extended servitude of any kind that exploits another's indebtedness and compromises human freedom. The spirit of the commandment is more forcefully stated in 24:7 and deemed a capital offense. On a higher level, this mandate speaks to the opportunistic abuse of one's neighbor, especially the powerful over the powerless (1 Sam 12:1-12; 1 Kgs 21:1-16).

give you all the commandments, the statutes and the ordinances; you must teach them, that they may observe them in the land I am giving them to possess.

³²Be careful, therefore, to do as the LORD, your God, has commanded you, not turning aside to the right or to the left, ³³but following exactly the way that the LORD, your God, commanded you that you may live and prosper, and may have long life in the land which you are to possess.

6 ¹This then is the commandment, the statutes and the ordinances, which the LORD, your God, has commanded that you be taught to observe in the land you are about to cross into to possess, ²so that you, that is, you, your child, and your grandchild, may fear the LORD, your God, by keeping, as long as you live, all his statutes and commandments which I enjoin on you, and thus have long life. ³Hear then, Israel, and be careful to observe them, that it may go well with you and that you may increase greatly; for the LORD, the God of your ancestors, promised you a land flowing with milk and honey.

The eighth commandment (v. 20) forbids false witness in order to preserve an Israelite's reputation and legal rights in the community. Harmony in human relations requires telling the truth, especially before the court. Hence, Israelite law prescribes the sworn testimony of two or three witnesses against a defendant (19:15; cf. Dan 13:52-59; Matt 18:16). The psalms cry out for a just hearing (Pss 4:2; 10:3-10).

The ninth and tenth commandments (v. 21) speak, respectively, to coveting a neighbor's wife and material possessions. These laws preserve the Israelite's spouse and property from loss through theft or scheming. The most powerful example of coveting another's wife in the Old Testament is David's adultery with Bathsheba (2 Sam 11:1-5). One should note that Deuteronomy distinguishes the wife from material property and uses a distinct verb for her; compare verse 21 with Exodus 20:17.

The promulgation of the Ten Commandments concludes with an exhortation to obedience. Why should one obey? The reasons are clear. As 5:22 states, Moses brings down tablets of chiseled stone from the Lord, tablets given to him apart from the people. These tablets contain the statutes and decrees to be lived in the Promised Land flowing with milk and honey. Observance is the key to long life in the land. Such is the motivation for the human obligation to observe the decrees with which the covenant is expressed.

The Great Commandment. ⁴Hear, O Israel! The LORD is our God, the LORD alone! ⁵Therefore, you shall love the LORD, your God, with your whole heart, and with your whole being, and with your whole strength. ⁶Take to heart these words which I command you today. ⁷Keep repeating them to your children. Recite them when you are at home and when you are away, when you lie down and when you get up. ⁸Bind them on your arm as a sign and let them be as a pendant on your forehead. ⁹Write them on the doorposts of your houses and on your gates.

Fidelity in Prosperity. ¹⁰When the LORD, your God, brings you into the land which he swore to your ancestors, to Abraham, Isaac, and Jacob, that he would give you, a land with fine, large cities that you did not build, ¹¹with houses full of goods of all sorts that you did not garner, with cisterns that you did not dig, with vineyards and olive groves that you did not plant; and when, therefore, you eat and are satisfied, ¹²be careful not to forget the LORD, who brought you out of the land of Egypt, that house of slavery. ¹³The LORD, your God, shall you fear; him shall you serve, and by his name shall you swear. ¹⁴You shall not go after other gods, any of the gods of the surrounding peoples—¹⁵for the LORD, your God who is in your midst, is a passionate God—lest the anger of the LORD, your God, flare up against you and he destroy you from upon the land.

¹⁶You shall not put the LORD, your God, to the test, as you did at Massah. ¹⁷But keep the commandments of the LORD, your God, and the decrees and the statutes he has commanded you. ¹⁸Do

6:4-25 The great commandment

The Shema (the word *shĕmaʿ* is a Hebrew imperative, which means "Hear!") reiterates the Lord's claim on Israel. However one chooses to translate the exclusivity or oneness of God in verse 4, Israel's covenant relationship is highlighted in this exhortation. Further, love of God in verse 5 is intimately tied to the heart, the seat of intellect and will in Semitic thought. The Deuteronomic theology of love expressed here pervades the entire book. It is out of the Lord's first love of Israel that the nation finds its self-understanding (4:37-40; 7:6-8; 10:15). Such affection is rooted in the Lord as God of the ancestors and is echoed in the gospels (Matt 22:37-39; Mark 12:29-31). Further, the soul is not conceived as an isolated entity that survives after death but a principle of life in all its forms. The soul (the same Hebrew word is sometimes translated as "spirit" or "being") bespeaks a needy humanity full of appetites, desires, and mortality (Job 6:7; Isa 29:8). Strength reflects a single-minded zeal to fulfill the Lord's will.

The call to teach future generations is also part of the commandment. To "keep repeating them" (v. 7; the word literally means to "sharpen" or "whet") to your children expresses getting to the heart of the matter with what is right and good in the sight of the LORD, that it may go well with you, and you may enter in and possess the good land which the LORD promised on oath to your ancestors, [19]driving all your enemies out of your way, as the LORD has promised.

Instruction to Children. [20]Later on, when your son asks you, "What do these decrees and statutes and ordinances mean?" which the LORD, our God, has enjoined on you, [21]you shall say to your son, "We were once slaves of Pharaoh in Egypt, but the LORD brought us out of Egypt with a strong hand [22]and wrought before our eyes signs and wonders, great and dire, against Egypt and against Pharaoh and his whole house. [23]He brought us from there to bring us in and give us the land he had promised on oath to our ancestors. [24]The LORD commanded us to observe all these statutes in fear of the LORD, our God, that we may always have as good a life as we have today. [25]This is our justice before the LORD, our God: to observe carefully

no ambiguity. Indeed, teaching children is a repeated mandate in Deuteronomy because Moses' speeches communicate rights and obligations that span generations (6:2; 20-25; 32:46-47). The details in verses 8-9 are metaphorical but become in early Judaism the phylacteries (leather bands with attached boxes worn on the left arm and forehead during prayer) and the *mezuzah* (a receptacle placed on the right-hand outer doorjamb which contains words from Deuteronomy).

The rewards of fidelity (vv. 10-19) are more than a reprise of previous statements in Deuteronomy. They serve as a bridge between the great Shema and the instructions to children because what the Lord commands must be lived out and passed on. In this light, what would arrival in the land mean in terms of gift and responsibility? As a gift, the land means reaping benefits at no great labor or cost. As responsibility, the narrative harks back to the Deuteronomic theology of remembering/forgetting. The mention of cisterns, vineyards, and olives is quaintly artful in the narrative. These three motifs refer to abundance in the land. Cisterns denote security through the availability of channeled and potable water (2 Kgs 18:31-32; Isa 36:16-17). The vineyard is a sign of divine blessing and a refuge to the widow, orphan, and resident alien in need (24:21-22; see Lev 19:10). Sharing the fruits of the vineyard is informed by the remembrance of having once been slaves in Egypt. Elsewhere in the Old Testament the vineyard is a metaphor for Israel itself (Isa 5:1-7). The olive tree is hardy, growing well even in rocky soil and, like the vineyard, a source of sustenance for those in need (24:20). The olive and its multipurpose oil represent all the traditional staples of the Promised Land: grain, wine, and oil (7:13; cf. 30:9).

this whole commandment he has enjoined on us."

7 Destruction of the Nations in the Land. ¹When the LORD, your God, brings you into the land which you are about to enter to possess, and removes many nations before you—the Hittites, Girgashites, Amorites, Canaanites, Perizzites, Hivites, and Jebusites, seven nations more numerous and powerful than you—²and when the LORD, your God, gives them over to you and you defeat them, you shall put them under the ban. Make no covenant with them and do not be gracious to them. ³You shall not intermarry with them, neither giving your daughters to their sons nor taking their daughters for your sons. ⁴For they would turn your sons from following me to serving other gods, and

then the anger of the LORD would flare up against you and he would quickly destroy you.

⁵But this is how you must deal with them: Tear down their altars, smash their sacred pillars, chop down their asherahs, and destroy their idols by fire. ⁶For you ▶ are a people holy to the LORD, your God; the LORD, your God, has chosen you from all the peoples on the face of the earth to be a people specially his own. ⁷It was not because you are more numerous than all the peoples that the LORD set his heart on you and chose you; for you are really the smallest of all peoples. ⁸It was because the LORD loved you and ▶ because of his fidelity to the oath he had sworn to your ancestors, that the LORD brought you out with a strong hand and redeemed you from the house of slavery,

7:1-26 Victory over the enemy

The text offers readers a striking example of the vagaries of war and conquest. Taking no prisoners is a military option that reaches its lowest level in genocide. But here the emphasis is more theological than historical. For example, the doom of the enemy protects the Israelites from possible intermarriage with them (v. 3). The social institution of marriage is a perennial litmus test of the current social climate, whether dealing with political opportunism (see 1 Kgs 11:1-8), cultural bias, or lovers who break from tradition. In sum, whatever else it is about, this text deals with the issue of whether my child can or should marry a person of another race, nationality, or religion.

7:1-11 The identity of Israel

The identity and cultic integrity of Israel are highlighted here (cf. Exod 34:11-16). The prohibition against making covenants or showing mercy to other peoples relates to Israel's holiness (v. 6), a status which implies that they must be somehow set apart in a special way. Holiness is an intrinsic characteristic of God (Exod 3:5; Isa 6:3) and requires harsh judgment on priests who abuse their cultic responsibilities via apostasy (Hos 4:4-19).

from the hand of Pharaoh, king of Egypt. ⁹Know, then, that the LORD, your God, is God: the faithful God who keeps covenant mercy to the thousandth generation toward those who love him and keep his commandments, ¹⁰but who repays with destruction those who hate him; he does not delay with those who hate him, but makes them pay for it. ¹¹Therefore carefully observe the commandment, the statutes and the ordinances which I command you today.

Blessings of Obedience. ¹²As your reward for heeding these ordinances and keeping them carefully, the LORD, your God, will keep with you the covenant mercy he promised on oath to your ancestors. ¹³He will love and bless and multiply you; he will bless the fruit of your womb and the produce of your soil, your grain and wine and oil, the young of your herds and the offspring of your flocks, in the land which he swore to your ancestors he would give you. ¹⁴You will be blessed above all peoples; no man or woman among you shall be childless nor shall your livestock be barren. ¹⁵The LORD will remove all sickness from you; he will not afflict you with any of the malignant diseases that you know from Egypt, but will leave them with all those who hate you.

¹⁶You shall consume all the peoples which the LORD, your God, is giving over to you. You are not to look on them with pity, nor serve their gods, for that would be a snare to you. ¹⁷If you say to yourselves, "These nations are more nu-

---

Israel's self-understanding is intimately associated with its covenant relationship with God. Israel is not worthy on its own merits but chosen out of love. They are in a strict sense the Lord's property (v. 6) and observing the commandments is a constant duty (v. 11). This self-understanding underpins all Old Testament theology and informs Christian identity as well (Rom 8:28-39).

7:12-15 The blessings of obedience

The motif of blessing punctuates these verses. Blessing is intrinsically related to fertility and by extension is related to all prosperity in the created order (Gen 1:28; 12:1-3; Num 6:22-27; Ps 127:3-5). Ideally, no family is childless, no livestock barren. Blessing is also relational, i.e., one can bless or be blessed in anticipation of some benefit that fosters goodness and well-being. Absence of disease is also connected to blessing. Infidelity brings on maladies of all sorts (28:58-62). Health is peace (Hebrew: *shālôm*) and associated with covenant loyalty.

7:16-26 The Lord as victor

Israel is encouraged not to fear in the face of its enemies. The imagery in these verses recalls the exodus from Egypt, especially details in the Song of the Sea (Exod 15:14-16). The enemy will panic in the face of the Lord's

merous than we. How can we dispossess them?" ¹⁸do not be afraid of them. Rather, remember clearly what the LORD, your God, did to Pharaoh and to all Egypt: ¹⁹the great testings which your own eyes have seen, the signs and wonders, the strong hand and outstretched arm with which the LORD, your God, brought you out. The same also will he do to all the peoples of whom you are now afraid. ²⁰Moreover, the LORD, your God, will send hornets among them, until those who are left and those who are hiding from you are destroyed. ²¹Therefore, do not be terrified by them, for the LORD, your God, who is in your midst, is a great and awesome God. ²²He will remove these nations before you little by little. You cannot finish with them quickly, lest the wild beasts become too numerous for you. ²³The LORD, your God, will give them over to you and throw them into utter panic until they are destroyed. ²⁴He will deliver their kings into your power,

that you may make their names perish from under the heavens. No one will be able to stand up against you, till you have destroyed them. ²⁵The images of their gods you shall destroy by fire. Do not covet the silver or gold on them, nor take it for yourselves, lest you be ensnared by it; for it is an abomination to the LORD, your God. ²⁶You shall not bring any abominable thing into your house, so as to be, like it, under the ban; loathe and abhor it utterly for it is under the ban.

8 God's Care. ¹Be careful to observe this whole commandment that I enjoin on you today, that you may live and increase, and may enter in and possess the land which the LORD promised on oath to your ancestors. ²Remember how for these forty years the LORD, your God, has directed all your journeying in the wilderness, so as to test you by affliction, to know what was in your heart: to keep his commandments, or not. ³He therefore ▶

---

incomparable power and suffer defeat amid Israel's victory. The command not to covet idols of silver or gold is intrinsic to Israelite law and theology. Idol worship is an abomination as seen in the incident of the golden calf (9:7-21; cf. Exod 32), because idols represent the religions of the surrounding nations, something that compromises holiness as being "set apart."

8:1-20 The temptations of prosperity

This chapter reiterates the Deuteronomic theology of remembering/forgetting and the temptations of the land. Observance demands ongoing recollection of God's mighty deeds on behalf of Israel, specifically the wandering in the desert with its tests of faith and divine sustenance by miraculous food and drink.

The temptations of prosperity relate to a universal aspect of human nature. Guaranteed security leads to laxity as time goes on because of the false presumption that it has always been so and will always be so. Smug

let you be afflicted with hunger, and then fed you with manna, a food unknown to you and your ancestors, so you might know that it is not by bread alone that people live, but by all that comes forth from the mouth of the LORD. ⁴The clothing did not fall from you in tatters, nor did your feet swell these forty years. ⁵So you must know in your heart that, even as a man disciplines his son, so the LORD, your God, disciplines you. ⁶Therefore, keep the commandments of the LORD, your God, by walking in his ways and fearing him.

Cautions About Prosperity. ⁷For the LORD, your God, is bringing you into a good country, a land with streams of water, with springs and fountains welling up in the hills and valleys, ⁸a land of wheat and barley, of vines and fig trees and pomegranates, of olive trees and of honey, ⁹a land where you will always have bread and where you will lack nothing, a land whose stones contain iron and in whose hills you can mine copper. ¹⁰But when you have eaten and are satisfied, you must bless the LORD, your God, for the good land he has given you. ¹¹Be careful not to forget the LORD, your God, by failing to keep his commandments and ordinances and statutes which I enjoin on you today: ¹²lest, when you have eaten and are satisfied, and have built fine houses and lived in them, ¹³and your herds and flocks have increased, your silver and gold has increased, and all your property has increased, ¹⁴you then become haughty of heart and forget the LORD, your God, who brought you out of the land of Egypt, that house of slavery; ¹⁵he guided you through the vast and terrible wilderness with its saraph serpents and scorpions, its parched and waterless ground; he brought forth water for you from the flinty rock ¹⁶and fed you in the wilderness with manna, a food unknown to your ancestors, that he might afflict you and test you, but also make you prosperous in the end. ¹⁷Otherwise, you might say in your heart, "It is my own power and the strength of my own hand that has got me this wealth." ¹⁸Remember then the LORD, your God, for he is the one who gives you the power to get wealth, by fulfilling, as he has now done,

---

self-assurance becomes more pervasive as successive generations enjoy unthreatened comfort (v. 14), so remembering a time of want is essential to true religion. Each generation must embrace the stories which are told over and over: "My father was a refugee Aramean . . ." (26:5; cf. Exod 12:26-27). Such humble beginnings, fraught with danger, contrast with the dream of the Promised Land and its securities.

The terrain is depicted as well-watered, with grain and fruits, olive trees, and honey. Such bounty can be wrongly accredited to human ingenuity and accomplishment, not cooperation in covenant with God. Israel must remember and retell each generation that the Lord is the master of the arable land, providing the rainfall to replenish the soil (11:10-12; cf. Gen 8:22).

the covenant he swore to your ancestors. [19]But if you do forget the Lord, your God, and go after other gods, serving and bowing down to them, I bear witness to you this day that you will perish utterly. [20]Like the nations which the Lord destroys before you, so shall you too perish for not listening to the voice of the Lord, your God.

9 **Unmerited Success.** [1]Hear, O Israel! You are now about to cross the Jordan to enter in and dispossess nations greater and stronger than yourselves, having large cities fortified to the heavens, [2]the Anakim, a people great and tall. You yourselves know of them and have heard it said of them, "Who can stand up against the Anakim?" [3]Know, then, today that it is the Lord, your God, who will cross over before you as a consuming fire; he it is who will destroy them and subdue them before you, so that you can dispossess and remove them quickly,

as the Lord promised you. [4]After the Lord, your God, has driven them out of your way, do not say in your heart, "It is because of my justice the Lord has brought me in to possess this land, and because of the wickedness of these nations the Lord is dispossessing them before me." [5]No, it is not because of your justice or the integrity of your heart that you are going in to take possession of their land; but it is because of their wickedness that the Lord, your God, is dispossessing these nations before you and in order to fulfill the promise he made on oath to your ancestors, Abraham, Isaac, and Jacob. [6]Know this, therefore: it is not because of your justice that the Lord, your God, is giving you this good land to possess, for you are a stiff-necked people.

The Golden Calf. [7]Remember and do not forget how you angered the Lord, your God, in the wilderness. From the

---

9:1-29 Israel's stubbornness

The chapter is punctuated by repeated themes and motifs: possession of the land in place of the enemy, divine commitment to ancestral promises, rebellion occasioning divine anger, fire, forty days and forty nights, etc.

9:1-6 The Lord's fidelity

The opening verses hark back to themes already addressed, e.g., the fear of the Anakim (1:28), and highlight that Israel cannot boast of its own merits, for the people are habitually stiff-necked (vv. 6, 13, 27) and rebellious (vv. 7, 23, 24). The Lord will drive out the enemy because of their pagan wickedness and the promises made to Israel's ancestors. The Lord and Israel work together in reaching victory, a detail noted in verse 3.

9:7-29 The intercession of Moses

This section presents a touching portrait of Moses, a multifaceted character in Israelite theology. He appeals on behalf of the people and wants to set things right. The Israelites are reminded of the golden calf debacle

day you left the land of Egypt until you came to this place, you have been rebellious toward the LORD. ⁸At Horeb you so provoked the LORD that he was angry enough to destroy you, ⁹when I had gone up the mountain to receive the stone tablets of the covenant which the LORD made with you. Meanwhile I stayed on the mountain forty days and forty nights; I ate no food and drank no water. ¹⁰The LORD gave me the two stone tablets inscribed, by God's own finger, with a copy of all the words that the LORD spoke to you on the mountain from the midst of the fire on the day of the assembly. ¹¹Then, at the end of the forty days and forty nights, when the LORD had given me the two stone tablets, the tablets of the covenant, ¹²the LORD said to me, Go down from here now, quickly, for your people whom you have brought out of Egypt are acting corruptly; they have already turned aside from the way I commanded them and have made for themselves a molten idol. ¹³I have seen now how stiff-necked this people is, the LORD said to me. ¹⁴Let me be, that I may destroy them and blot out their name from under the heavens. I will then make of you a nation mightier and greater than they.

¹⁵When I had come down again from the blazing, fiery mountain, with the two tablets of the covenant in both my hands, ¹⁶I saw how you had sinned against the LORD, your God, by making for yourselves a molten calf. You had already turned aside from the way which the LORD had commanded you. ¹⁷I took hold of the two tablets and with both hands

---

and Moses' intercession at that juncture (Exod 32). The pattern of pronouns is striking in the narrative. The discourse begins with "you," i.e., Israel, leaving Egypt and subsequent moments of rebellion in the wilderness, then moves to "I," i.e., Moses' intercessory fasting, prayer, and reception of the Ten Commandments. The section concludes with these two pronouns juxtaposed to highlight the sin of the people and the intervention of Moses (vv. 18-19). Even Aaron, who so much embodies Israelite priesthood, is indicted. Moses stands alone as righteous amid their rebellion; he is ever Israel's intercessor in the face of divine anger (cf. Exod 32:11-14; Sir 45:1-5).

The motif of forty days and nights deserves comment, given its fourfold repetition (vv. 9, 11, 18, 25). Numbers in the Bible relate only secondarily to counting. Forty represents a complete cycle or major event, such as the flood (Gen 7:12), the wandering in the wilderness (Exod 16:35; Num 14:20-23), and Jesus' temptation in the desert (Luke 4:1-13). Here the number forty marks the sequence of events that culminate in Moses' prayerful intercession in the wake of divine anger (vv. 25-29). Moses is on the mountain and then descends after forty days; he lies prostrate for forty days in intercession for the sinful people.

cast them from me and broke them before your eyes. [18]Then, as before, I lay prostrate before the LORD for forty days and forty nights; I ate no food, I drank no water, because of all the sin you had committed in the sight of the LORD, doing wrong and provoking him. [19]For I dreaded the fierce anger of the LORD against you: his wrath would destroy you. Yet once again the LORD listened to me. [20]With Aaron, too, the LORD was deeply angry, and would have destroyed him; but I prayed for Aaron also at that time. [21]Then, taking the calf, the sinful object you had made, I burnt it and ground it down to powder as fine as dust, which I threw into the wadi that went down the mountainside.

[22]At Taberah, at Massah, and at Kibroth-hattaavah likewise, you enraged the LORD. [23]And when the LORD sent you up from Kadesh-barnea saying, Go up and take possession of the land I have given you, you rebelled against this command of the LORD, your God, and would not believe him or listen to his voice. [24]You have been rebels against the LORD from the day I first knew you.

[25]Those forty days, then, and forty nights, I lay prostrate before the LORD, because he had threatened to destroy you. [26]And I prayed to the Lord and said: O Lord GOD, do not destroy your people, the heritage you redeemed in your greatness and have brought out of Egypt with your strong hand. [27]Remember your servants, Abraham, Isaac, and Jacob. Do not look upon the stubbornness of this people nor upon their wickedness and sin, [28]lest the land from which you have brought us say, "The LORD was not able to bring them into the land he promised them, and out of hatred for them, he brought them out to let them die in the wilderness." [29]They are your people and your heritage, whom you have brought out by your great power and with your outstretched arm.

Further, anthropomorphic images of God inform the narrative. The finger of God etches the stone tablets (v. 10; cf. Exod 8:15; 31:18), and God's outstretched arm frees Israel from bondage (v. 29; cf. Exod 6:6). Such images reveal divine presence and intervention, while also limiting any depiction of God in iconography.

Moses' prayer concludes this section. The tone may seem manipulative to modern canons of piety, i.e., the plea "remember . . . lest" (vv. 27-28). The Lord's honor is at stake before other gods and nations. Such intercession is not foreign to Old Testament prayer (Exod 32:11-14; Num 14:15-16; Ps 22:3-6). The prayer also illustrates the theology of divine freedom in that the Lord can have a change of heart. In the Scriptures cause and effect, mercy and justice, are all mysteries that defy a systematic theology. Such is the case with Abel's offering being accepted over that of Cain (Gen 4:3-4) and David's selection from among his brothers as the Lord's anointed (1 Sam 16:11-13).

10 ¹At that time the LORD said to me, Cut two stone tablets like the first ones and come up the mountain to me. Also make an ark out of wood. ²I will write upon the tablets the words that were on the tablets that you broke, and you shall place them in the ark. ³So I made an ark of acacia wood, and cut two stone tablets like the first ones, and went up the mountain with the two tablets in my hand. ⁴The LORD then wrote on the tablets, as he had written before, the ten words that the LORD had spoken to you on the mountain from the midst of the fire on the day of the assembly; and the LORD gave them to me. ⁵Then I turned and came down from the mountain, and placed the tablets in the ark I had made. There they have remained, as the LORD commanded me.

⁶The Israelites set out from Beeroth Bene-jaakan for Moserah; Aaron died there and was buried. His son Eleazar succeeded him as priest. ⁷From there they set out for Gudgodah, and from Gudgodah for Jotbathah, a region where there is water in the wadies. ⁸At that time the LORD set apart the tribe of Levi to carry the ark of the covenant of the LORD, to stand before the LORD to minister to him, and to bless in his name, as they have done to this day. ⁹For this reason, Levi has no hereditary portion with his relatives; the LORD himself is his portion, as the LORD, your God, promised him.

¹⁰Meanwhile I stayed on the mountain as I did before, forty days and forty nights, and once again the LORD listened to me. The LORD was unwilling to destroy you. ¹¹The LORD said to me, Go now and set out at the head of the people, that they may enter in and possess the land that I swore to their ancestors I would give them.

The Lord's Majesty and Compassion. ¹²Now, therefore, Israel, what does the LORD, your God, ask of you but to fear

---

10:1-11 The ark of the covenant

New stone tablets of the Ten Commandments are commissioned, to be deposited in the ark of the covenant. This chest of acacia wood represented the divine presence on journeys and in the cult (Num 10:35-36; 1 Sam 5), but by the time of Solomon references to the ark all but vanish. Symbolically, the ark represents God's going forth with the people, especially in battle. Besides the Ten Commandments, the ark reportedly contained Aaron's staff and a vessel of manna from the wilderness. It had rings on its sides through which poles were inserted for easy transport (Exod 25:10-16).

10:12–11:9 The great equation

This section presents the gist of Deuteronomic theology. What does the Lord ask? The answer is fourfold: that one love the Lord, fear the Lord, keep the commandments, and walk in the Lord's ways (10:12-13).

the LORD, your God, to follow in all his ways, to love and serve the LORD, your God, with your whole heart and with your whole being, [13]to keep the commandments and statutes of the LORD that I am commanding you today for your own well-being? [14]Look, the heavens, even the highest heavens, belong to the LORD, your God, as well as the earth and everything on it. [15]Yet only on your ancestors did the LORD set his heart to love them. He chose you, their descendants, from all the peoples, as it is today. [16]Circumcise therefore the foreskins of your hearts, and be stiff-necked no longer. [17]For the LORD, your God, is the God of gods, the Lord of lords, the great God, mighty and awesome, who has no favorites, accepts no bribes, [18]who executes justice for the orphan and the widow, and loves the resident alien, giving them food and clothing. [19]So you too should love the resident alien, for that is what you were in the land of Egypt. [20]The LORD, your God, shall you fear, and him shall you serve; to him hold fast and by his name shall you swear. [21]He is your praise; he is your God, who has done for you those great and awesome things that your own eyes have seen. [22]Seventy strong your ancestors went down to Egypt, and now the LORD, your God, has made you as numerous as the stars of heaven.

11 Recalling the Wonders of the Lord. [1]Love the LORD, your God, therefore, and keep his charge, statutes, ordinances, and commandments always. [2]Recall today that it was not your children, who have neither known nor seen the discipline of the LORD, your God— his greatness, his strong hand and outstretched arm; [3]the signs and deeds he wrought in the midst of Egypt, on Pharaoh, king of Egypt, and on all his land; [4]what he did to the Egyptian army and to their horses and chariots, engulfing them in the waters of the Red Sea as they pursued you, so that the LORD destroyed them even to this day; [5]what he did for you in the wilderness until you came to this place; [6]and what he did to the Reubenites Dathan and Abiram, sons of Eliab, when the earth opened its mouth and swallowed them up out of the midst of Israel, with their families and tents and every living thing that belonged to them—[7]but it was you who saw with your own eyes all these great deeds that the LORD has done.

The Gift of Rain. [8]So keep all the commandments I give you today, that

---

The circumcision of the heart is a metaphor for repentance and a new way of living. As stated above (see 6:5-6), the heart is the seat of the will and intellect, so its "circumcision" describes an irreversible change of heart that draws one closer to God. This inward transformation supersedes the outward mark of physical circumcision that serves as a visible symbol of religious identity. Humans judge by appearance; God sees into the heart.

The orphan, widow, and alien cited together in a triad (10:18) stand for the disenfranchised in society who depend on the kindness of others (14:28-29; cf. Exod 22:20-23; 26:12; Ps 10:14-18).

you may be strong enough to enter in and take possession of the land that you are crossing over to possess, ⁹and that you may have long life on the land which the LORD swore to your ancestors he would give to them and their descendants, a land flowing with milk and honey. ¹⁰The land you are to enter and possess is not like the land of Egypt from which you have come, where you would sow your seed and then water it by hand, as in a vegetable garden. ¹¹No, the land into which you are crossing to take possession is a land of mountains and valleys that drinks in rain from the heavens, ¹²land which the LORD, your God, looks after; the eyes of the LORD, your God, are upon it continually through the year, from beginning to end.

¹³If, then, you truly listen to my commandments which I give you today, loving and serving the LORD, your God, with your whole heart and your whole being, ¹⁴I will give the seasonal rain to your land, the early rain and the late rain, that you may have your grain, wine and oil to gather in; ¹⁵and I will bring forth grass in your fields for your animals. Thus you may eat and be satisfied. ¹⁶But be careful lest your heart be so lured away that you serve other gods and bow down to them. ¹⁷For then the anger of the LORD will flare up against you and he will close up the heavens, so that no rain will fall, and the soil will not yield its crops, and you will soon perish from the good land the LORD is giving you.

Need for Fidelity. ¹⁸Therefore, take these words of mine into your heart and soul. Bind them on your arm as a sign, and let them be as a pendant on your forehead. ¹⁹Teach them to your children,

11:10-17 The gift of rain

The Nile River of Egypt (some 4,000 miles in length from its source to its estuary) creates a climate that contrasts strongly with the seasonal rainfall in Palestine. Egypt receives little rain and depends on the flow of water along the Nile and irrigation for sustenance. The river's annual flooding deposits silt along its banks to promote agriculture. Before modern dam construction, desert lay beyond the banks of the Nile. The imagery here extols the gift of the seasonal cycle "that drinks in rain from the heavens" (v. 11). However, as with the flow of the Nile, unpredictable weather patterns create cycles of feast and famine. The theological point of the rain motif is its connection with loyalty to the covenant. The temptation of apostasy to pagan gods (e.g., the Canaanite Baal was god of the thunderstorm) brings disaster on the Israelites; the Lord will withhold rain and thus blessing (vv. 16-17).

11:18-32 The need for fidelity

This statute harks back to the great Shema. The Lord alone is God of Israel; all other gods are as naught, so decision for the Lord is at the heart

Moses receiving the Ten Commandments in Hebrew, Latin, and Greek. A 1512 picture in the Ann Ronan Picture Library.

speaking of them when you are at home and when you are away, when you lie down and when you get up, [20]and write them on the doorposts of your houses and on your gates, [21]so that, as long as the heavens are above the earth, you and your children may live on in the land which the Lord swore to your ancestors he would give them.

[22]For if you are careful to observe this entire commandment I am giving you, loving the Lord, your God, following his ways exactly, and holding fast to him, [23]the Lord will dispossess all these nations before you, and you will dispossess nations greater and mightier than yourselves. [24]Every place where you set foot shall be yours: from the wilderness and the Lebanon, from the Euphrates River to the Western Sea, shall be your territory. [25]None shall stand up against you; the Lord, your God, will spread the fear and dread of you through any land where you set foot, as he promised you.

Blessing and Curse. [26]See, I set before you this day a blessing and a curse: [27]a blessing for obeying the commandments of the Lord, your God, which I give you today; [28]a curse if you do not obey the commandments of the Lord, your God, but turn aside from the way I command you today, to go after other gods, whom you do not know. [29]When the Lord, your God, brings you into the land which you are to enter and possess, then on Mount Gerizim you shall pronounce the blessing, on Mount Ebal, the curse. [30](These are beyond the Jordan, on the other side of the western road in the land of the Canaanites who live in the Arabah, opposite Gilgal beside the oak of Moreh.) [31]Now you are about to cross the Jordan to enter and possess the land which the Lord, your God, is giving you. When, therefore, you take possession of it and settle there, [32]be careful to observe all the statutes and ordinances that I set before you today.

---

of this exhortation and will result in either blessing or curse. Blessing reinforces the rain motif discussed previously, i.e., the blessing of creation by means of rain and other positive forces of nature represents order brought out of chaos, seasonal harmony, and fruitfulness in the land. Obedience brings blessing, but disobedience brings a perennial curse.

12:1–26:19 Deuteronomic law

This lengthy section elaborates on a wide variety of legislation, creating what many refer to as the Deuteronomic Code. These laws build on the Ten Commandments and the great Shema; these two guiding principles are used to inform more specific circumstances. The legislation is not systematic and is rooted in traditional values handed down over generations. The integrity of this unit is indicated by the inclusion (12:1 and 26:16-19) that enjoins Israel to observe these statutes and decrees as a people of divine promise and set apart in holiness to serve the Lord.

B. The Deuteronomic Code

12 **One Center of Worship.** [1]These are the statutes and ordinances which you must be careful to observe in the land which the LORD, the God of your ancestors, has given you to possess, throughout the time you live on its soil. [2]Destroy entirely all the places where the nations you are to dispossess serve their gods, on the high mountains, on the hills, and under every green tree. [3]Tear down their altars, smash their sacred pillars, burn up their asherahs, and chop down the idols of their gods, that you may destroy the very name of them from that place.

[4]That is not how you are to act toward the LORD, your God. [5]Instead, you shall seek out the place which the LORD, your God, chooses out of all your tribes and designates as his dwelling to put his name there. There you shall go, [6]bringing your burnt offerings and sacrifices, your tithes and personal contributions, your votive and voluntary offerings, and the firstlings of your herds and flocks. [7]There, too, in the presence of the LORD, your God, you and your families shall eat and rejoice in all your undertakings, in which the LORD, your God, has blessed you.

[8]You shall not do as we are doing here today, everyone doing what is right in their own sight, [9]since you have not yet reached your resting place, the heritage which the LORD, your God, is giving

---

12:1-19 Conquest and centralization

The narrative is divided into three parts (vv. 1-7; 8-12; 13-19) and punctuated by the threefold repetition of "rejoice" (vv. 7, 12, 18). Merriment is a celebration of the divine blessing for the individual and the community. At the center of this section the theme of rest is highlighted (vv. 9-10). Successful conquest and prosperity in the land are celebrated in the Psalter as well (Pss 21; 110).

Conquest and centralization of the cult evoke a variety of associations. Conquest realizes the Lord's promise of the land to Abraham and his descendants and the curse of Canaan (Gen 9:25-27; 13:15). Thus it also reflects the extermination or banishment of indigenous peoples, a theme that is troublesome to the modern reader, given the Holocaust, ethnic cleansing, and other events, but theologically the issue is the integrity of true religion and covenant fidelity. Pure worship cannot tolerate the deification of natural phenomena, the carving of images that compromise divine freedom, and the manipulation of God by incantations, fertility rites, child sacrifice, etc. Centralization, a key theme in Deuteronomy and related Deuteronomic literature, bespeaks purity and integrity of worship. A plethora of holy sites imitates the multiplicity of Canaanite local shrines and increases the

you. ¹⁰But after you have crossed the Jordan and dwell in the land which the LORD, your God, is giving you as a heritage, when he has given you rest from all your enemies round about and you live there in security, ¹¹then to the place which the LORD, your God, chooses as the dwelling place for his name you shall bring all that I command you: your burnt offerings and sacrifices, your tithes and personal contributions, and every special offering you have vowed to the LORD. ¹²You shall rejoice in the presence of the LORD, your God, with your sons and daughters, your male and female slaves, as well as with the Levite within your gates, who has no hereditary portion with you.

possibility of dabbling in pagan practices. In Israelite theology no place is inherently sacred; a site is holy because of the divine presence and communication which take place there. At the burning bush the ground was holy because the Lord was present, and Moses took off his sandals in reverential awe (Exod 3:5; cf. Isa 6:1-4).

12:1-7 Destruction of Canaanite sanctuaries

This mandate is riddled with verbs of utter destruction: destroy, tear down, smash, burn up, shatter. Ultimately, the goal is to suppress any memory of pagan practice (v. 3), an irony in light of Israel's own Deuteronomic theology of remembering for itself.

The place of the Lord's dwelling (v. 5) refers in a veiled way to the centralized cult in Jerusalem, an anachronism here, given that David's reign is still in the future (2 Sam 5:6-12). Likewise, the list of sacrificial offerings reflects a more defined cult.

12:8-12 Centralization

After crossing the Jordan, Israel will move toward more centralization of the cult. In principle, no longer can someone simply do what seems right (v. 8; literally, "what is right in one's own eyes." Compare that phrase with "What is right in the sight of the LORD," 13:19; 21:9). That such centralization took place is not a mere fiction. Efforts to consolidate the cult are reflected in the programs of Hezekiah and Josiah (2 Kgs 18:4; 23:19-20). Most probably, historical events such as war, loss of territory, and economic crisis were the driving forces behind centralization of the cult, but centralization had a deeper theological meaning. For instance, it allowed for precise seasonal celebrations on an annual basis by all the people, including covenant renewal under a defined priestly heritage (18:1-8).

¹³Be careful not to sacrifice your burnt offerings in any place you like, ¹⁴but offer them in the place which the LORD chooses in one of your tribal territories; there you shall do what I command you.

Profane and Sacred Slaughter. ¹⁵However, in any of your communities you may slaughter and eat meat freely, according to the blessing that the LORD, your God, has given you; the unclean as well as the clean may eat it, as they do the gazelle or the deer. ¹⁶Only, you shall not eat of the blood, but must pour it out on the ground like water. ¹⁷Moreover, you may not, in your own communities, partake of your tithe of grain or wine or oil, of the firstborn of your herd or flock, of any offering you have vowed, of your voluntary offerings, or of your personal contributions. ¹⁸These you must eat in the presence of the LORD, your God, in the place that the LORD, your God, chooses, along with your son and daughter, your male and female slave, and the Levite within your gates; and there, in the presence of the LORD, you shall rejoice in all your undertakings. ¹⁹Be careful, also, that you do not neglect the Levite as long as you live in your land.

²⁰After the LORD, your God, has enlarged your territory, as he promised

---

12:13-19 The nature of right sacrifice

A distinction is made between the ordinary and the ritual slaughter of animals, a detail inserted at this point because of the centralization of the cult in place of multiple shrines. In a sense all slaughter of meat in the ancient world was "sacred" in that it provided nourishment. Universally, the act of saying grace before meals gives thanks for bounty from God. Although the narrative describes abundance of meat as a blessing (v. 15), the daily diet of the ancient world was more dependent on grains. Meat was by and large reserved for special banquets (Exod 16:12; Amos 6:4; Dan 10:3). Partaking of the blood of slaughtered animals was taboo because blood was essential to life and a vicarious means of atonement (v. 23; cf. Lev 17:11). Further, the references to grain-wine-oil, the firstborn, and vowed or voluntary offerings add to the breadth of what constituted a sacred meal. As noted above, the grain, wine, and oil formed a triad of staples in the ancient Near East; the firstborn held a privileged position; and the disenfranchised (widow, orphan, and resident alien), along with the Levites, deserved charity and hospitality (12:12; 26:11-12). All these blessings are cause to make merry and rejoice.

12:20-28 Further comments

These verses expand on the preceding section and elaborate further on the sacred nature of blood. Blood is not to be consumed with its flesh, a

45

you, and you think, "I will eat meat," as it is your desire to eat meat, you may eat it freely; [21]and if the place where the LORD, your God, chooses to put his name is too far, you may slaughter in the manner I have commanded you any of your herd or flock that the LORD has given you, and eat it freely in your own community. [22]You may eat it as you would the gazelle or the deer: the unclean and the clean eating it together. [23]But make sure that you do not eat of the blood; for blood is life; you shall not eat that life with the flesh. [24]Do not eat of the blood, therefore, but pour it out on the ground like water. [25]Do not eat of it, that you and your children after you may prosper for doing what is right in the sight of the LORD. [26]However, any sacred gifts or votive offerings that you may have, you shall bring with you to the place which the LORD chooses, [27]and there you must sacrifice your burnt offerings, both the flesh and the blood, on the altar of the LORD, your God; of your other sacrifices the blood indeed must be poured out against the altar of the LORD, your God, but their flesh you may eat.

[28]Be careful to heed all these words I command you today, that you and your descendants after you may forever prosper for doing what is good and right in the sight of the LORD, your God.

Warning Against Abominable Practices. [29]When the LORD, your God, cuts down from before you the nations you

---

point reiterated four times (vv. 23-25). Such abstention assures prosperity in the land and is rooted in the primeval history, the instruction to Noah in the covenant (Gen 9:4; cf. Acts 15:20, 29). However, blood which has been set apart is an acceptable component in certain circumstances. A blood ritual seals the covenant with the Lord (Exod 24:3-8). Atonement involves blood (Lev 16:15) and is also found in the ordination sacrifice and priestly consecration (Exod 29:20). Verse 28 is a fitting conclusion to this section as it reiterates the benefits of observance for later generations. Such conduct is right in the sight (literally, "in the eyes") of the Lord. The eyes of God see all; idols have eyes but cannot see (Pss 115:4-5; 135:15-16).

12:29-31 The lure of idols

These verses hark back to 12:1-7 and emphasize that Israel's victory is essentially the work of God. As already warned, a temptation in the Promised Land will be attraction to pagan idols (11:16). The Bible paints a thoroughly negative picture of Canaanite religion, and the prophets berate Israelite kings for adopting foreign images and rituals. Paganism is an abomination (v. 31) because it includes such sins as eating unclean animals, unchaste behavior, idol worship, and human sacrifice. All are contrary to true religion.

are going in to dispossess, and you have dispossessed them and are settled in their land, ³⁰be careful that you not be trapped into following them after they have been destroyed before you. Do not inquire regarding their gods, "How did these nations serve their gods, so I might do the same." ³¹You shall not worship the LORD, your God, that way, because they offered to their gods every abomination that the LORD detests, even burning their sons and daughters to their gods.

13 **Penalties for Enticing to Idolatry.** ¹Every word that I command you, you shall be careful to observe, neither adding to it nor subtracting from it.

²If there arises in your midst a prophet or a dreamer who promises you a sign or wonder, ³saying, "Let us go after other gods," whom you have not known, "and let us serve them," and the sign or wonder foretold to you comes to pass, ⁴do not listen to the words of that prophet or that dreamer; for the LORD, your God, is testing you to know whether you really love the LORD, your God, with all your heart and soul. ⁵The LORD, your God, shall you follow, and him shall you fear; his commandments shall you observe, and to his voice shall you listen; him you shall serve, and to him you shall hold fast. ⁶But that prophet or that dreamer shall be put to death, because, in order to lead you astray from the way which the LORD, your God, has commanded you to take, the prophet or dreamer has spoken apostasy against the LORD, your God, who brought you out of the land of Egypt and redeemed you from the house of slavery. Thus shall you purge the evil from your midst.

⁷If your brother, your father's child or your mother's child, your son or

13:1-19 Leading astray

The chapter is punctuated by the threefold repetition of "straying" (literally, "to thrust out, or banish"; vv. 6, 11, 14). This verb is rooted in shepherding where the flocks serve as a vivid metaphor for straying (Jer 23:2; 50:17). By extension the verb suggests seduction of the faithful away from the right path. Each usage here highlights a particular circumstance, i.e., false prophesy, enticement to idolatry by a family member, and being led astray by the broader community.

Given this background, the prophet and the dreamer come under scrutiny because their vocation includes admonishing the sinner and calling the errant people back to covenant fidelity. Deuteronomic law offers a fine and often overlooked nuance to the characteristics of true prophecy. What comes to pass in prophecy is not as important as the message's conformity to true religion as outlined in Deuteronomy. False prophecy may come true, but the event is a test from the Lord. Finally, family members can have a negative impact by enticing a relative to paganism (vv. 7-10; cf. Matt 10:34-38).

daughter, your beloved spouse, or your intimate friend entices you secretly, saying, "Come, let us serve other gods," whom you and your ancestors have not known, [8]any of the gods of the surrounding peoples, near to you or far away, from one end of the earth to the other: [9]do not yield or listen to any such person; show no pity or compassion and do not shield such a one, [10]but kill that person. Your hand shall be the first raised to put such a one to death; the hand of all the people shall follow. [11]You shall stone that person to death, for seeking to lead you astray from the LORD, your God, who brought you out of the land of Egypt, out of the house of slavery. [12]And all Israel shall hear of it and fear, and never again do such evil as this in your midst.

[13]If you hear it said concerning one of the cities which the LORD, your God, gives you to dwell in, [14]that certain scoundrels have sprung up in your midst and have led astray the inhabitants of their city, saying, "Come, let us serve other gods," whom you have not known, [15]you must inquire carefully into the matter and investigate it thoroughly. If you find that it is true and an established fact that this abomination has been committed in your midst, [16]you shall put the inhabitants of that city to the sword, placing the city and all that is in it, even its livestock, under the ban. [17]Having heaped up all its spoils in the middle of its square, you shall burn the city with all its spoils as a whole burnt offering to the LORD, your God. Let it be a heap of ruins forever, never to be rebuilt. [18]You shall not hold on to anything that is under the ban; then the LORD will turn from his burning anger and show you mercy, and in showing you mercy multiply you as he swore to your ancestors, [19]because you have listened to the voice of the LORD, your God, keeping all his commandments, which I give you today, doing what is right in the sight of the LORD, your God.

Perhaps the most powerful warning relates to communal apostasy (vv. 13-19). The abominations of false prophecy and familial misguidance crescendo into social sin on a grand scale. The narrative depicts citywide apostasy (v. 14) that results in vast retribution (v. 16). This calls to mind the Tower of Babel where the escalation of sin in the primeval history came to affect all human life (Gen 11; cf. Jonah 3 on the conversion of Nineveh). Yet this section ends on a positive note. Heeding the Lord's voice brings mercy and renewed blessing (vv. 18-19), a reward for keeping the commandments.

In sum, Deuteronomy offers timeless laws that warn against being led astray by human voices that may not reflect divine will. Deuteronomic law, written down and proclaimed to the assembly, fosters remembrance and long life in the land (32:45-47).

14 **Improper Mourning Rites.** ¹You are children of the LORD, your God. You shall not gash yourselves nor shave the hair above your foreheads for the dead. ²For you are a people holy to the LORD, your God; the LORD, your God, has chosen you from all the peoples on the face of the earth to be a people specially his own.

Clean and Unclean Animals. ³You shall not eat any abominable thing. ⁴These are the animals you may eat: the ox, the sheep, the goat, ⁵the deer, the gazelle, the roebuck, the wild goat, the ibex, the antelope, and the mountain sheep. ⁶Any among the animals that has divided hooves, with the foot cloven in two, and that chews the cud you may eat. ⁷But you shall not eat any of the following that chew the cud or have cloven hooves: the camel, the hare, and the rock badger, which indeed chew the cud, but do not have divided hooves; they are unclean for you. ⁸And the pig, which indeed has divided hooves, with cloven foot, but does not chew the cud, is unclean for you. Their flesh you shall not eat, and their dead bodies you shall not touch.

⁹These you may eat, of all that live in the water: whatever has both fins and scales you may eat, ¹⁰but all those that lack either fins or scales you shall not eat; they are unclean for you.

¹¹You may eat all clean birds. ¹²But you shall not eat any of the following: the griffon vulture, the bearded vulture, the black vulture, ¹³the various kites and falcons, ¹⁴all kinds of crows, ¹⁵the eagle

---

14:1-29 Children of the Lord

To be children of the Lord (v. 1) involves a right relationship. Specifically, it demands obedience, a challenge emphasized throughout the Scriptures (21:18-21; cf. Sir 3:1-16; Matt 21:28-31). When properly observed, rituals, dietary laws, tithing, and other demands demonstrate fidelity to the covenant and stewardship of the created order.

14:1-2 Ritual custom

In the ancient Near East canons of mourning often involved an emotional display with wailing, the chanting of dirges, rending of garments, wearing of sackcloth, sitting in ashes, and self-mutilation. Shaving the head and gashing the body are expressly prohibited because they mirror Canaanite rituals (1 Kgs 18:28; Jer 47:5; Ezek 9:14-15).

14:3-21 Dietary laws

The exact names of these forbidden foods are obscure in Hebrew and their English equivalents are not certain. Whatever the rules of clean/unclean, dietary laws distinguish one's religious identity apart from other faiths. In conjunction with the blood laws cited above, certain kinds of animals are not to be consumed at all. Fish with fins and scales, as well

owl, the kestrel, the long-eared owl, all species of hawks, [16]the little owl, the screech owl, the barn owl, [17]the horned owl, the osprey, the cormorant, [18]the stork, any kind of heron, the hoopoe, and the bat. [19]All winged insects are also unclean for you and shall not be eaten. [20]Any clean winged creatures you may eat.

[21]You shall not eat the carcass of any animal that has died of itself; but you may give it to a resident alien within your gates to eat, or you may sell it to a foreigner. For you are a people holy to the LORD, your God.

You shall not boil a young goat in its mother's milk.

Tithes. [22]Each year you shall tithe all the produce of your seed that grows in the field; [23]then in the place which the LORD, your God, chooses as the dwelling place of his name you shall eat in his presence the tithe of your grain, wine and oil, as well as the firstlings of your herd and flock, that you may learn always to fear the LORD, your God. [24]But if, when the LORD, your God, blesses you, the journey is too much for you and you are not able to bring your tithe, because the place which the LORD, your God, chooses to put his name is too far for you, [25]you may exchange the tithe for money, and with the money securely in

as quadrupeds with cloven hooves and chewing cud, are acceptable (Lev 11:3-12). Clean animals reflect order in creation (birds, fish, land animals; Gen 1:26), unlike hybrid creatures that represent lack of distinction and embody the primordial chaos before creation. Some commentators suggest that food hygiene is at the root of some forbidden items, given the lack of refrigeration and preservatives. Whatever the exact origin of these dietary laws, their observance shows that Israel belongs to the Lord and is set apart in holiness.

14:22-29 Tithes

The practice of tithing (offering a tenth of one's income) is an enduring institution used to support political and sacral activities. In the ancient world when distance prohibited bringing an offering of grain-wine-oil and firstlings to the sanctuary, a cash donation was acceptable (Lev 27:30-33). Care of the poor by tithing adds a charitable dimension to the practice. Such a duty is to be carried out with joy and happiness, returning in kind what God has given in creation (Sir 35:7-14). Support of the Levites (v. 29) reflects consideration of those with no inheritance who serve in the sacral realm (Num 18:21-32; Neh 10:37-38).

Such right conduct brings divine blessing. Once again Deuteronomy reiterates that blessing is intimately related to fertility, expansion, and well-being in life. It also acknowledges that bounty is a gift in a Promised Land that ultimately belongs to the Lord.

hand, go to the place which the LORD, your God, chooses. ²⁶You may then exchange the money for whatever you desire, oxen or sheep, wine or beer, or anything else you want, and there in the presence of the LORD, your God, you shall consume it and rejoice, you and your household together. ²⁷But do not neglect the Levite within your gates, for he has no hereditary portion with you.

²⁸At the end of every third year you shall bring out all the tithes of your produce for that year and deposit them within your own communities, ²⁹that the Levite who has no hereditary portion with you, and also the resident alien, the orphan and the widow within your gates, may come and eat and be satisfied; so that the LORD, your God, may bless you in all that you undertake.

15 **Debts and the Poor.** ¹At the end of every seven-year period you shall have a remission of debts, ²and this is the manner of the remission. Creditors shall remit all claims on loans made to a neighbor, not pressing the neighbor, one who is kin, because the LORD's remission has been proclaimed. ³You may press a foreigner, but you shall remit the claim on what your kin owes to you. ⁴However, since the LORD, your God, will bless you abundantly in the land the LORD, your God, will give you to possess as a heritage, there shall be no one of you in need ⁵if you but listen to the voice of the LORD, your God, and carefully observe this entire commandment which I enjoin on you today. ⁶Since the LORD, your God, will bless you as he promised, you will lend to many nations, and borrow from none; you will rule over many nations, and none will rule over you.

⁷If one of your kindred is in need in any community in the land which the

15:1-23 Ownership and relaxation of debt

The chapter discusses laws regarding a variety of issues: the waiving of debts, emancipation of Hebrew slaves, and the offering of animal firstlings. These regulations are intimately linked to sabbath ideals, particularly the value of a regular day of rest and relief from indentured service.

15:1-11 No one in need

Ideally, no Israelite should be in need, although in reality there would always be needy people in the land (Matt 26:11). Tensions between ideals and realities in life mandate the periodic relaxation of debts on a communal level. The seven-year period enjoined here is rooted in the principle of protecting the poor from economic exploitation and endless service in paying off debts (Exod 22:24-26; Lev 25:35-38). This sabbatical year does not benefit foreigners, and its exact nature remains a point of debate. Is the debt canceled, or is it merely suspended for a grace period? Whatever the case, the effort to ease debts reflects the great Deuteronomic call to love one's neighbor.

LORD, your God, is giving you, you shall not harden your heart nor close your hand against your kin who is in need. ⁸Instead, you shall freely open your hand and generously lend what suffices to meet that need. ⁹Be careful not to entertain the mean thought, "The seventh year, the year of remission, is near," so that you would begrudge your kin who is in need and give nothing, and your kin would cry to the LORD against you and you would be held guilty. ¹⁰When you give, give generously and not with a stingy heart; for that, the LORD, your God, will bless you in all your works and undertakings. ¹¹The land will never lack for needy persons; that is why I command you: "Open your hand freely to your poor and to your needy kin in your land."

Hebrew Slaves. ¹²If your kin, a Hebrew man or woman, sells himself or herself to you, he or she is to serve you for six years, but in the seventh year you shall release him or her as a free person. ¹³When you release a male from your service, as a free person, you shall not send him away empty-handed, ¹⁴but shall weigh him down with gifts from your flock and threshing floor and wine press; as the LORD, your God, has blessed you, so you shall give to him. ¹⁵For remember that you too were slaves in the land of Egypt, and the LORD, your God, redeemed you. That is why I am giving you this command today. ¹⁶But if he says to you, "I do not wish to leave you," because he loves you and your household, since he is well off with you, ¹⁷you shall take an awl and put it through his ear into the door, and he shall be your slave forever. Your female slave, also, you shall treat in the same way. ¹⁸Do not be reluctant when you let them go free, since the service they have given you for six years was worth twice a hired laborer's salary; and the LORD, your God, will bless you in everything you do.

Firstlings. ¹⁹You shall consecrate to the LORD, your God, every male firstling born in your herd and in your flock. You

15:12-18 Slavery

The seven-year period of relaxation continues in regard to Hebrew slaves. This commandment is rooted in the abiding recollection of Israel having been ransomed from slavery in Egypt. Such indentured servitude is always one way of paying off a debt, but the practice is ripe for abuse. An Israelite's integrity and identity with the whole body of the Israelite nation transcend monetary debt, so freed slaves deserve assistance in making the transition from involuntary service back to freedom. Not being sent away "empty-handed" (vv. 13-14) recalls the flight of the Israelites from Egypt when the Hebrews went on their way laden with gifts (Exod 3:22; 12:36).

15:19-23 Firstlings

Offering the firstlings of the flocks or the first fruits of the harvest is an ancient institution. The firstlings belong to God and are offered back in

shall not work the firstlings of your cattle, nor shear the firstlings of your flock. [20]In the presence of the LORD, your God, you shall eat them year after year, you and your household, in the place that the LORD will choose. [21]But if a firstling has any defect, lameness or blindness, any such serious defect, you shall not sacrifice it to the LORD, your God, [22]but in your own communities you may eat it, the unclean and the clean eating it together, as you would a gazelle or a deer. [23]Only, you must not eat of its blood; you shall pour it out on the ground like water.

16 **Feast of the Passover.** [1]Observe the month of Abib by keeping the Passover of the LORD, your God, since it was in the month of Abib that the LORD, your God, brought you out of Egypt by night. [2]You shall offer the Passover sacrifice from your flock and your herd to the LORD, your God, in the place the LORD will choose as the dwelling place of his name. [3]You shall not eat leavened bread with it. For seven days you shall eat with it only unleavened bread, the bread of affliction, so that you may remember as long as you live the day you left the land of Egypt; for in hurried flight you left the land of Egypt. [4]No leaven is to be found with you in all your territory for seven days, and none of the meat which you sacrificed on the evening of the first day shall be kept overnight for the next day.

[5]You may not sacrifice the Passover in any of the communities which the LORD, your God, gives you; [6]only at the

---

anticipation of ongoing fertility. For Israel the first Passover in Egypt initiated this practice in that the firstborn males of Israel were saved during the tenth plague by the blood of a lamb sprinkled on the lintel and doorjamb of the house (Exod 12:22-23). Except under special circumstances, a firstborn ranks first in inheritance. Blemished firstborn animals are handled differently (vv. 21-22; cf. 17:1).

16:1-17 The great feasts

Religions typically observe annual celebrations that embody their collective experience of God and give cause to assemble ritually. For Israel the calendar includes Passover (Unleavened Bread), Weeks, and Booths. These feasts are cited elsewhere in the Pentateuch (Exod 23:14-17; 34:18-23; Lev 23; Num 28–29) and in Deuteronomy are connected to the central sanctuary.

Passover is the celebration of the wandering shepherds' firstlings and is rooted in an annual nomadic feast where the blood of the slaughtered animal was used to assure safe passage during migration. Unleavened Bread recognizes the barley harvest and the leaven used by the settled farmer. Despite their distinct origin, both are integrated into the exodus from Egypt (Exod 12:1-28).

place which the LORD, your God, will choose as the dwelling place of his name, and in the evening at sunset, at the very time when you left Egypt, shall you sacrifice the Passover. [7]You shall cook and eat it at the place the LORD, your God, will choose; then in the morning you may return to your tents. [8]For six days you shall eat unleavened bread, and on the seventh day there shall be a solemn assembly for the LORD, your God; on that day you shall do no work.

Feast of Weeks. [9]You shall count off seven weeks; begin to count the seven weeks from the day when the sickle is first put to the standing grain. [10]You shall then keep the feast of Weeks for the LORD, your God, and the measure of your own voluntary offering which you will give shall be in proportion to the blessing the LORD, your God, has given you. [11]You shall rejoice in the presence of the LORD, your God, together with your son and daughter, your male and female slave, and the Levite within your gates, as well as the resident alien, the orphan, and the widow among you, in the place which the LORD, your God, will choose as the dwelling place of his name. [12]Remember that you too were slaves in Egypt, so carry out these statutes carefully.

Feast of Booths. [13]You shall celebrate the feast of Booths for seven days, when you have gathered in the produce from your threshing floor and wine press. [14]You shall rejoice at your feast, together with your son and daughter, your male and female slave, and also the Levite, the resident alien, the orphan and the widow within your gates. [15]For seven days you shall celebrate this feast for the LORD,

---

The feast of Weeks (also called Pentecost; Acts 2:10) is another agricultural feast, a spring agricultural feast rooted in the farmer's offering of the first fruits of the barley harvest. Deuteronomy gives precision to this observance by placing it seven weeks after the sickle is put to the standing grain, broadening what was probably an individual offering of the harvest into a national pilgrimage.

The feast of Booths (also called Tabernacles, Succoth, or Ingathering) is an autumn celebration, especially of such fruits as grapes, olives, and dates at the end of the annual harvest season. Traditionally, Booths related to Israel's wandering in the wilderness and living in tents. This memory occasions a time of celebration that lasts for a week, from sabbath to sabbath (cf. Lev 23:39-43; Neh 8:13-18). Temporary shelters are erected in the orchards while the harvesters make merry over the agricultural bounty. Speaking of a much later time, Josephus says that its observance included menorah lamps, music, dancing, and generous libations of water and wine. The feast became associated with messianic hope and restoration of the fortunes of Israel via Hanukkah, also called the feast of Dedication (1 Macc 4:54-59).

your God, in the place which the LORD will choose; since the LORD, your God, has blessed you in all your crops and in all your undertakings, you will be full of joy.

¹⁶Three times a year, then, all your males shall appear before the LORD, your God, in the place which he will choose: at the feast of Unleavened Bread, at the feast of Weeks, and at the feast of Booths. They shall not appear before the LORD empty-handed, ¹⁷but each with his own gift, in proportion to the blessing which the LORD, your God, has given to you.

Justice. ¹⁸In all the communities which the LORD, your God, is giving you, you shall appoint judges and officials throughout your tribes to administer true justice for the people. ¹⁹You must not distort justice: you shall not show partiality; you shall not take a bribe, for a bribe blinds the eyes even of the wise and twists the words even of the just. ²⁰Justice, justice alone shall you pursue, so that you may live and possess the land the LORD, your God, is giving you.

Illicit Worship. ²¹You shall not plant an asherah of any kind of wood next to the altar of the LORD, your God, which you will build; ²²nor shall you erect a sacred pillar, such as the LORD, your God, hates.

17 ¹You shall not sacrifice to the LORD, your God, an ox or a sheep with any serious defect; that would be an abomination to the LORD, your God.

²If there is found in your midst, in any one of the communities which the LORD, your God, gives you, a man or a woman who does evil in the sight of the LORD, your God, and transgresses his covenant, ³by going to serve other gods, by bowing down to them, to the sun or the moon or any of the host of heaven, contrary to my command; ⁴and if you are told or hear of it, you must investigate it thoroughly. If the truth of the matter is established that this abomination has been committed in Israel, ⁵you shall bring the man or the woman who has done this evil deed out to your gates and stone the man or the woman to death. ⁶Only on the testimony of two or three witnesses shall a person be put to death; no one shall be put to death on the testimony of only one witness. ⁷The hands of the witnesses shall be the first raised to put the person to death, and afterward the hands of all the people. Thus shall you purge the evil from your midst.

16:18–18:22 Leadership in Israel

This section describes leadership roles over the course of Israelite history, beginning with the Judges. The material in 16:21–17:7 may appear to interrupt the flow of the narrative, but it does establish canons of right judgment through dutiful leadership. Further, we learn that pagan practices and blemished sacrifices are unacceptable in the cult. The worship of celestial bodies patently contradicts the Israelite theology of creation (Gen 1:14-19; Ps 19:1). False witness is also dismissed as contrary to the Ten Commandments and related laws (5:20; 19:15; cf. Exod 20:16). Fidelity and right judgment foster peace, social order, and long life in the land.

Judges. ⁸If there is a case for judgment which proves too baffling for you to decide, in a matter of bloodshed or of law or of injury, matters of dispute within your gates, you shall then go up to the place which the LORD, your God, will choose, ⁹to the levitical priests or to the judge who is in office at that time. They shall investigate the case and then announce to you the decision. ¹⁰You shall act according to the decision they announce to you in the place which the LORD will choose, carefully observing everything as they instruct you. ¹¹You shall carry out the instruction they give you and the judgment they pronounce, without turning aside either to the right or left from the decision they announce to you. ¹²Anyone who acts presumptuously and does not obey the priest who officiates there in the ministry of the LORD, your God, or the judge, shall die. Thus shall you purge the evil from Israel. ¹³And all the people, on hearing of it, shall fear, and will never again act presumptuously.

The King. ¹⁴When you have come into the land which the LORD, your God, is giving you, and have taken possession of it and settled in it, should you then decide, "I will set a king over me, like all the surrounding nations," ¹⁵you may indeed set over you a king whom the LORD, your God, will choose. Someone from among your own kindred you may set over you as king; you may not set over

16:18-20; 17:8-13 Judges

The role of the judge in the Scriptures is not univocal. In the historical books (Josh–2 Kgs) this was the institution that provided the Israelites with leadership before the monarchy. This is clearest in the beginning of the book of Judges where these leaders are not simply justices in legal matters. They are military leaders who rescue errant Israel from the enemy and oversee a time of peace. Deuteronomic theology colors this portrait: Israel sins, is punished, cries out for help, and the Lord sends a judge to the rescue. A time of peace then follows.

In the book of Deuteronomy the tasks of judges are more strictly legal in nature, and they are presented as vigilant protectors of the law whose verdicts must be accepted. Levitical priests are included as a balance to the judges. In sum, Israelite tradition enjoins judges not to take bribes (16:19) and to defend the triad of needy persons: the widow, orphan, and resident alien.

17:14-20 Kings

The origins of the monarchy in Israel are complicated. Old Testament tradition preserves both pro- and anti-monarchy traditions (1 Sam 8–18),

you a foreigner, who is no kin of yours. [16]But he shall not have a great number of horses; nor shall he make his people go back again to Egypt to acquire many horses, for the LORD said to you, Do not go back that way again. [17]Neither shall he have a great number of wives, lest his heart turn away, nor shall he accumulate a vast amount of silver and gold. [18]When he is sitting upon his royal throne, he shall write a copy of this law upon a scroll from the one that is in the custody of the levitical priests. [19]It shall remain with him and he shall read it as long as he lives, so that he may learn to fear the LORD, his God, and to observe carefully all the words of this law and these statutes, [20]so that he does not exalt himself

and the rise of kingship is associated with the Philistine threat and the need for a more consolidated government, over and above the tribal federation. The people want a king like all the surrounding nations (1 Sam 8:19-20) and eventually get one. Unique to Israelite monarchy is the monarch's subordination to the Lord as a vassal king. He is subject to the law and expected to embody covenant ideals and mete out justice impartially (v. 20). Israel's kings are never made into gods.

The extent to which the portrayal of the Israelite monarchy found in the Bible reflects objective history is debated. Some scholars think there is less history here than theology, but the ancients did not understand "history" in the modern sense of the word, i.e., objective recorded events in chronological order.

Curiously, the narrative highlights certain royal prerogatives that remain in check, i.e., horses and wives (vv. 16-17). These items have a metaphorical value that should not be overlooked. As is the case even today, horses are much associated with the upper class, because the wealthy can afford their care and maintenance. The Philistine threat cited above comes into play because of the recollection of their chariots and horsemen against King Saul (1 Sam 13:5; cf. 2 Sam 15:1-6 on Absalom). Further, horses represent the hidden dangers of military prowess and royal privilege, i.e., human pride. Deuteronomy insists that reliance on the Lord supersedes "horse and chariot," a tenet sung in Israel's worship and prophecy (Pss 20:8; 33:16-19; 76:7-8; 147:10; Isa 43:16-17; Ezek 26:7).

Many wives represent polygamy and the luxury of a harem. Such is the issue behind Absalom's invasion of his father's harem in the sight of the people (2 Sam 16:20-22). This action is tantamount to pretensions to the throne of David his father.

over his kindred or turn aside from this commandment to the right or to the left, and so that he and his descendants may reign long in Israel.

18 **Priests.** ¹The levitical priests, the whole tribe of Levi, shall have no hereditary portion with Israel; they shall eat the fire offerings of the LORD and the portions due to him. ²They shall have no heritage among their kindred; the LORD himself is their heritage, as he has told them. ³This shall be the due of the priests from the people: those who are offering a sacrifice, whether an ox or a sheep, shall give the priest the shoulder, the jowls and the stomach. ⁴The first fruits of your grain, your wine, and your oil, as well as the first shearing of your flock, you shall also give him. ⁵For the LORD, your God, has chosen him out of all your tribes to be in attendance to minister in the name of the LORD, him and his descendants for all time.

⁶When a Levite goes from one of your communities anywhere in Israel in which he has been residing, to visit, as his heart may desire, the place which the LORD will choose, ⁷and ministers there in the name of the LORD, his God, like all his fellow Levites who stand before the LORD there, he shall receive the same portions to eat, along with his stipends and patrimony.

18:1-8 Levites and priests

The history of the Israelite priesthood is complex. Religions define themselves by concepts of sacred space, times and seasons, and chosen representatives who serve as intermediaries between the human and divine. Here the Levites are portrayed as dependent on the beneficence of others, devoid of property and assets (vv. 6-8). Whatever the actual historical background, the Deuteronomic concern about priestly rights stems from the suppression of local shrines and the centralization of the cult in Jerusalem. In Deuteronomy the levitical priests gain prominence (v. 8; 27:9-10; 31:9-13).

Levites also embody a perennial value, that being sponsored and subsidized by others is not a burden on the religious community but a gift that frees a person to serve the wider community without extraneous burdens. Fiscal self-sufficiency is not the litmus test of dignified ministry in any age. By definition benefactors support persons and groups that depend on their largesse. At the heart of such service is the acknowledgement of one's ultimate dependence on God (cf. Luke 12:22-34). By the time of Chronicles, Levites would be given a more defined history, claiming a clear genealogy from the ancient tribe of Levi (1 Chr 6).

Prophets. [9]When you come into the land which the LORD, your God, is giving you, you shall not learn to imitate the abominations of the nations there. [10]Let there not be found among you anyone who causes their son or daughter to pass through the fire, or practices divination, or is a soothsayer, augur, or sorcerer, [11]or who casts spells, consults ghosts and spirits, or seeks oracles from the dead. [12]Anyone who does such things is an abomination to the LORD, and because of such abominations the LORD, your God, is dispossessing them before you. [13]You must be altogether sincere with the LORD, your God. [14]Although these nations whom you are about to dispossess listen to their soothsayers and diviners, the LORD, your God, will not permit you to do so.

[15]A prophet like me will the LORD, your God, raise up for you from among your own kindred; that is the one to whom you shall listen. [16]This is exactly what you requested of the LORD, your God, at Horeb on the day of the assembly, when you said, "Let me not again hear the voice of the LORD, my God, nor see this great fire any more, or I will die." [17]And the LORD said to me, What they have said is good. [18]I will raise up for them a prophet like you from among their kindred, and will put my words into the mouth of the prophet; the prophet shall tell them all that I command. [19]Anyone who will not listen to my words which the prophet speaks in my name, I myself will hold accountable for it. [20]But if a prophet presumes to speak a word in my name that I have not commanded, or speaks in the name of other gods, that prophet shall die.

[21]Should you say to yourselves, "How can we recognize that a word is one the LORD has not spoken?", [22]if a prophet speaks in the name of the LORD but the word does not come true, it is a word the LORD did not speak. The prophet has spoken it presumptuously; do not fear him.

18:9-22 Prophets

Genuine prophecy is regulated in the Deuteronomic Code and viewed with a certain guardedness. Here the discussion picks up from 13:1-6 and its warning against false prophets. The narrative can be divided into two parts: vv. 9-14 and vv. 15-22, the latter building on the former prohibitions.

It is noteworthy how Moses is idealized as prophet par excellence (vv. 15, 18). Moses the prophet is one biblical portrait of Israel's exodus leader, but he was also thought of as liberator, priest, judge, model of humility, and privileged intimate of God. He speaks the word of the Lord and commands obedience. The task of Old Testament prophecy is characterized as one that ensures covenant fidelity and proclaims the word of God. Indeed, emphasis on the "word" from Moses punctuates verses 18-22. Obedience

19 **Cities of Refuge.** [1]When the LORD, your God, cuts down the nations whose land the LORD, your God, is giving you, and you have dispossessed them and settled in their cities and houses, [2]you shall set apart three cities in the land the LORD, your God, is giving you to possess. [3]You shall measure the distances and divide into three regions the land of which the LORD, your God, is giving you possession, so that every homicide will be able to find a refuge.

[4]This is the case of a homicide who may take refuge there and live: when someone strikes down a neighbor unintentionally and not out of previous hatred. [5]For example, if someone goes with a neighbor to a forest to cut wood, wielding an ax to cut down a tree, and its head flies off the handle and hits the neighbor a mortal blow, such a person may take refuge in one of these cities and live. [6]Should the distance be too great, the avenger of blood might in hot anger pursue, overtake, and strike the killer dead, even though that one does not deserve the death penalty since there had been no previous hatred; [7]for this reason I command you: Set apart three cities.

[8]But if the LORD, your God, enlarges your territory, as he swore to your ancestors, and gives you all the land he promised your ancestors he would give, [9]because you carefully observe this whole commandment which I give you today, loving the LORD, your God, and ever walking in his ways, then add three more cities to these three. [10]Thus, in the land which the LORD, your God, is giving you as a heritage, innocent blood will not be shed and you will not become guilty of bloodshed.

[11]However, if someone, hating a neighbor, lies in wait, attacks, and strikes

brings peace and prosperity; disobedience brings disaster, often via invasion by foreign adversaries. Such elements of the Deuteronomic theology of prophecy color other books as well (2 Kgs 17:13-18).

19:1-13 More on cities of refuge

Refer to 4:41-43 for a discussion of this provision in Deuteronomic law. The city of refuge protects a fugitive from indiscriminate vigilante justice and emotionally driven blood vengeance, especially from the traditional redeemer of blood (2 Sam 14:7).

The city of refuge is a sparsely attested but powerful theme in the Old Testament. Later rabbinic tradition elaborates on its provisions. The city should be near a water supply and street markets so that the refugee lacks nothing, in a populous district so that a cry for help can be heard, without any trafficking of arms or traps lest the avenger purchase his goods there. Elsewhere, refuge is depicted in the metaphors of the tent, rocky fastness, secure dwelling, or shelter (33:27-28; cf. Isa 33:16; Ps 142:5-6). Ultimately, God is our refuge (Ps 14:6; 71:7).

Palm tree in the Sinai area

the neighbor dead, and then flees to one of these cities, ¹²the elders of the killer's own city shall send and have the killer taken from there, to be handed over to the avenger of blood and slain. ¹³Do not show pity, but purge from Israel the innocent blood, so that it may go well with you.

Removal of Landmarks. ¹⁴You shall not move your neighbor's boundary markers erected by your forebears in the heritage that will be allotted to you in the land the LORD, your God, is giving you to possess.

False Witnesses. ¹⁵One witness alone shall not stand against someone in regard to any crime or any offense that may have been committed; a charge shall stand only on the testimony of two or three witnesses.

¹⁶If a hostile witness rises against someone to accuse that person of wrongdoing, ¹⁷the two parties in the dispute shall appear in the presence of the LORD, in the presence of the priests and judges in office at that time, ¹⁸and the judges must investigate it thoroughly. If the witness is a false witness and has falsely

19:14 Boundaries and landmarks

This small piece of legislation bespeaks the Deuteronomic theology of the land. No one can violate the inheritance of another by moving boundary markers. Ahab's seizure of Naboth's vineyard with the complicity of the notorious Jezebel is a good example of such abuse (1 Kgs 21). Deuteronomic theology emphasizes that landmarks and boundaries are a sacred value and related to the protection of inheritance (v. 14; 27:17). The Lord apportions the nations their inheritance (32:8). As the prophets proclaim, human greed cannot rationalize such injustice and avoid divine retribution (cf. Mic 2:2).

19:15-21 False witness

Prior to the benefit of modern forensic tools like fingerprinting and DNA analysis, the sworn testimony of witnesses has been a given in human history. In the Scriptures two or more firsthand witnesses were needed for conviction (17:6; cf. Num 35:30). Obviously, such a system is open to abuse. Perjury is difficult to prove when false witnesses conspire, and especially when they are considered pillars of the community. Such is the suspense of the Susanna tale (Dan 13). Hence, this statute takes a defensive stance and imposes harsh penalties for such obstruction of justice (vv. 16-19). False witness deserves the *lex talionis*: "eye for eye, tooth for tooth," i.e., retribution not excessive but equal to the injury. It remains debated whether this law is to be interpreted literally or is simply a guiding dictum in deciding cases.

accused the other, ¹⁹you shall do to the false witness just as that false witness planned to do to the other. Thus shall you purge the evil from your midst. ²⁰The rest shall hear and be afraid, and never again do such an evil thing as this in your midst. ²¹Do not show pity. Life for life, eye for eye, tooth for tooth, hand for hand, and foot for foot!

20 **Courage in War.** ¹When you go out to war against your enemies and you see horses and chariots and an army greater than your own, you shall not be afraid of them, for the LORD, your God, who brought you up from the land of Egypt, will be with you.

²When you are drawing near to battle, the priest shall come forward and speak to the army, ³and say to them, "Hear, O Israel! Today you are drawing near for battle against your enemies. Do not be weakhearted or afraid, alarmed or frightened by them. ⁴For it is the LORD, your God, who goes with you to fight for you against your enemies and give you victory."

⁵Then the officials shall speak to the army: "Is there anyone who has built a new house and not yet dedicated it? Let him return home, lest he die in battle and another dedicate it. ⁶Is there anyone who has planted a vineyard and not yet plucked its fruit? Let him return home, lest he die in battle and another pluck its fruit. ⁷Is there anyone who has betrothed a woman and not yet married her? Let him return home, lest he die in battle and another marry her." ⁸The officials

20:1-20 The rules of war

This legislation builds on 7:1-26 and anticipates further items (chs. 21–25). The opening section (vv. 1-4) once again recalls the Song of the Sea (Exod 15:1-18). The Israelites should not fear military prowess, for the Lord brought forth the Israelites from Egypt and continues to go forth with them into battle. Further, the call to hear (v. 3) reiterates the great Shema, i.e., if the Lord is God alone, live righteously and fear not the vagaries of war.

The following three sections build on this spirited introduction: exemption from military service (vv. 5-9), negotiating with the enemy (vv. 10-18), and the ecological impact of war (vv. 19-20). The narrative assumes a compassionate tone. Soldiers with a new home, vineyard, or wife are exempt from immediate military duty. A human value is celebrated here. Each person should enjoy property, marriage, and family before being put in harm's way. Even modern military law allows for compassionate leave, deferment from service because of siblings killed in battle, and other exemptions. One's name and inheritance should not cease to exist in the land, a violation often at the hands of those most empowered (2 Sam 12:9; 1 Kgs 21:3).

shall continue to speak to the army: "Is there anyone who is afraid and weak-hearted? Let him return home, or else he might make the hearts of his fellows melt as his does."

⁹When the officials have finished speaking to the army, military commanders shall be appointed over them.

Cities of the Enemy. ¹⁰When you draw near a city to attack it, offer it terms of peace. ¹¹If it agrees to your terms of peace and lets you in, all the people to be found in it shall serve you in forced labor. ¹²But if it refuses to make peace with you and instead joins battle with you, lay siege to it, ¹³and when the LORD, your God, delivers it into your power, put every male in it to the sword; ¹⁴but the women and children and livestock and anything else in the city—all its spoil—you may take as plunder for yourselves, and you may enjoy this spoil of your enemies, which the LORD, your God, has given you.

¹⁵That is how you shall deal with any city at a considerable distance from you, which does not belong to these nations here. ¹⁶But in the cities of these peoples that the LORD, your God, is giving you as a heritage, you shall not leave a single soul alive. ¹⁷You must put them all under the ban—the Hittites, Amorites, Canaanites, Perizzites, Hivites, and Jebusites—just as the LORD, your God, has commanded you, ¹⁸so that they do not teach you to do all the abominations that they do for their gods, and you thus sin against the LORD, your God.

Trees of a Besieged City. ¹⁹When you are at war with a city and have to lay siege to it for a long time before you capture it, you shall not destroy its trees by putting an ax to them. You may eat of them, but you must not cut them down. Are the trees of the field human beings, that they should be included in your siege? ²⁰However, those trees which you know are not fruit trees you may destroy. You may cut them down to build siege-works against the city that is waging war with you, until it falls.

The destruction of trees while laying siege (vv. 19-20) raises herme-neutical questions. At first glance, the preservation of fruit trees seems an agricultural nicety, speaking to the theology of ecology. However, one may ask a deeper question: Why and under what circumstances do trees supersede the value of human life? This point is all the more troubling in light of the mandate to kill the men, while holding women, children, and livestock as valuable booty (v. 13-14). Deuteronomy reflects the time in which it was written, but the book also speaks perennially to the violence of war, as well as the abuse of people who have suffered devastation and are zealous for retribution.

21 Absolution of Untraced Murder.

¹If the corpse of someone who has been slain is found lying in the open, in the land the Lᴏʀᴅ, your God, is giving you to possess, and it is not known who killed the person, ²your elders and judges shall go out and measure the distances to the cities that are in the neighborhood of the corpse. ³When it is established which city is nearest the corpse, the elders of that city shall take a heifer that has never been put to work or worn a yoke; ⁴the elders of that city shall bring the heifer down to a wadi with an everflowing stream at a place that has not been plowed or sown, and shall break the heifer's neck there in the wadi. ⁵The priests, the descendants of Levi, shall come forward, for the Lᴏʀᴅ, your God, has chosen them to minister to him and to bless in the name of the Lᴏʀᴅ, and every case of dispute or assault shall be for them to decide. ⁶Then all the elders of that city nearest the corpse shall wash their hands over the heifer whose neck was broken in the wadi, ⁷and shall declare, "Our hands did not shed this blood, and our eyes did not see the deed. ⁸Absolve, O Lᴏʀᴅ, your people Israel, whom you have redeemed, and do not let the guilt of shedding innocent blood remain in the midst of your people Israel." Thus they shall be absolved from the guilt of bloodshed, ⁹and you shall purge the innocent blood from your midst, and do what is right in the eyes of the Lᴏʀᴅ.

21:1–25:19 Various laws

This section contains a variety of laws, many of which apply general principles to specific problems. Such laws are couched in an "If . . . then" pattern. Compliance secures inheritance, long life, and prosperity in the land (21:9, 23; 22:7; 23:21; 25:15; 26:8-11).

21:1-9 The guilt of innocent blood

This law demands communal responsibility for a rural murder and links the crime to the nearest city. The slaughter of a heifer and the ritual hand washing by the elders atone for the offense. Special to this law is the prayer therein (vv. 7-8). The elders pray for absolution, noting that neither hand nor eye was involved, i.e., neither committing nor aiding and abetting the crime. In ancient anthropology the hand symbolizes responsibility. Hand washing is thus a declaration of innocence (Matt 27:24). Further, the eye is not understood in terms of light entering the body but a transmission outward from the person. Hence, vision intrinsically stems from the living being. God sees all (11:12), idols have eyes but cannot see (Pss 115:5; 135:16), and humans see God incompletely (Num 24:4; Jer 5:21). Deuteronomic laws regarding homicide remind the reader that the loss of human life is not an isolated event but a tragedy that impacts the entire community.

Marriage with a Female Captive. [10]When you go out to war against your enemies and the LORD, your God, delivers them into your power, so that you take captives, [11]if you see a beautiful woman among the captives and become so enamored of her that you wish to have her as a wife, [12]and so you take her home to your house, she must shave her head, cut her nails, [13]lay aside her captive's garb, and stay in your house, mourning her father and mother for a full month. After that, you may come to her, and you shall be her husband and she shall be your wife. [14]If later on you lose your liking for her, you shall give her her freedom, if she wishes it; you must not sell her for money. Do not enslave her, since you have violated her.

Rights of the Firstborn. [15]If a man has two wives, one loved and the other unloved, and if both the loved and the unloved bear him sons, but the firstborn is the son of the unloved wife: [16]when he comes to bequeath his property to his sons he may not consider as his firstborn the son of the wife he loves, in preference to the son of the wife he does not love, the firstborn. [17]On the contrary, he shall recognize as his firstborn the son of the unloved wife, giving him a double share of whatever he happens to own,

21:10-14 War brides

Although monogamy was the usual social practice for economic reasons in the ancient world, polygamy remained an option. In practice only monarchs and the wealthy could afford multiple wives, technically called polygyny. To the point, this rule of war is baldly sexist by modern standards. Women are among the spoils of war and objects of forced marriage. The one-month grace period is deemed a kindness (v. 13), but the fact that consummation of the marriage is imminent and the husband can easily dismiss her makes the grace period more a formality than anything gracious.

The high female mortality rate in the ancient world due to death in childbirth is often cited as a pretext for polygyny. The stipulation that the war bride assumes the status of an Israelite woman assures her technical freedom (v. 14). The best the modern reader can see here is a primitive effort to establish some military justice. However, protocols of warfare (e.g., the 1864 Geneva Convention) are never acted out judiciously when humans get caught up in the violence and mass carnage that are often involved.

21:15-17 The firstborn

Ancient laws tended to defer to the firstborn son. Canons of seniority and inheritance were involved, as well as maintaining family order. In Deuteronomic thought, parental favoritism and sibling rivalry must not supersede birthrights and due process.

since he is the first fruits of his manhood, and to him belong the rights of the first-born.

The Stubborn and Rebellious Son. [18]If someone has a stubborn and rebellious son who will not listen to his father or mother, and will not listen to them even though they discipline him, [19]his father and mother shall take hold of him and bring him out to the elders at the gate of his home city, [20]where they shall say to the elders of the city, "This son of ours is a stubborn and rebellious fellow who will not listen to us; he is a glutton and a drunkard." [21]Then all his fellow citizens shall stone him to death. Thus shall you purge the evil from your midst, and all Israel will hear and be afraid.

Corpse of a Criminal. [22]If a man guilty of a capital offense is put to death and you hang him on a tree, [23]his corpse shall not remain on the tree overnight. You must bury it the same day; anyone who is hanged is a curse of God. You shall not defile the land which the LORD, your God, is giving you as a heritage.

The firstborn is a grand motif in the Scriptures, extending even to animals. Such new life belongs to God as first fruits and is the focus of the tenth plague against Egypt (Exod 12:29-30; 13:2, 12-16). Israel itself is described as the Lord's firstborn (Exod 4:22; cf. Matt 1:25; Heb 12:23).

21:18-21 Family discord

This law seems excessive by modern standards, but the intent is maintaining good social order. Rebellious children reach beyond the family and impact on the entire community (cf. 21:1-9). The communal aspect brings town elders into the picture as mediators, and justice is meted out at the city gate (v. 19; cf. Josh 2:4; Ruth 4:1). In the best circumstances mediation settles the domestic dispute and avoids bloodshed. The death penalty is a communal event (v. 21). Stoning is a corporate act to purge an offense against the people and is often executed outside the town or city (Lev 17:5-7; 24:14). The gist of this legislation is that grievous and habitual sinning against family and community demands a communal response.

21:22-23 Hanging on a tree

The statute does not reflect hanging as a form of capital punishment but public exposure after execution. Such an act serves as a warning to others. The corpse is not to remain exposed overnight. Timely burial is dictated in Israelite law. Nonburial of the dead, even in time of war, or later desecration of a grave is an abomination (Tob 1:17-18; 4:3-4). The violent end of Jezebel, wife of Ahab, serves as an example of the desecration of a corpse (2 Kgs 9:30-37). She is humiliated and her memory erased in the land.

22 **Concern for the Neighbor.** ¹You shall not see your neighbor's ox or sheep going astray and ignore it; you must bring it back. ²If this neighbor does not live near you, or you do not know who the owner may be, take it to your own house and keep it with you until your neighbor claims it; then return it. ³You shall do the same with a donkey; you shall do the same with a garment; and you shall do the same with anything else which your neighbor loses and you happen to find. You may not ignore them.

⁴You shall not see your neighbor's donkey or ox fallen on the road and ignore it; you must help in lifting it up.

Various Precepts. ⁵A woman shall not wear a man's garment, nor shall a man put on a woman's clothing; for anyone who does such things is an abomination to the LORD, your God.

⁶If, while walking along, you come across a bird's nest with young birds or eggs in it, in any tree or on the ground, and the mother bird is sitting on them, you shall not take away the mother bird along with her brood. ⁷You must let the

22:1-4 Respect for livestock

Return of lost property is a universal value, especially when of high monetary or sentimental value (cf. Exod 23:4-5). The famous parable of the ewe lamb illustrates attachment to animals (2 Sam 12:1-6). Harmonious community life depends on respect for what belongs to others and rendering aid when necessary.

22:5 Rules of dress

Appropriate and fashionable dress is culturally conditioned and much associated with gender. In an oblique way, such order speaks to harmony in creation and is spoofed in burlesque when men and women wear one another's clothing or dress outlandishly. This law relates to other prohibitions that define accepted boundaries, e.g., kosher foods, clothing made of one thread, etc. Although the Scriptures offer no detailed record about men's and women's clothing, certain passages identify dress according to status and role (Gen 38:14; Isa 3:18-24).

22:6-7 Nestlings

This short precept speaks again to the theology of ecology and harks back to 20:19-20. Apart from modern sensitivities about the ethical treatment of animals, the spirit of the law is to ensure survival of the species. Taking only eggs or nestlings allows the mother to reproduce. In addition, the ancient world lacked our refined ornithological nomenclature and broke birds into three basic categories: kosher food, votive offerings, and forbidden food. Many names for birds cited in Bible translations are tentative.

mother go, taking only her brood, in order that you shall prosper and have a long life.

⁸When you build a new house, put a parapet around the roof, so that you do not bring bloodguilt upon your house if someone falls off.

⁹You shall not sow your vineyard with two different kinds of seed, or else its produce shall become forfeit, both the crop you have sown and the yield of the vineyard. ¹⁰You shall not plow with an ox and a donkey harnessed together. ¹¹You shall not wear cloth made from wool and linen woven together.

¹²You shall put tassels on the four corners of the cloak that you wrap around yourself.

22:8 Sound construction

Although not motivated by malice, involuntary manslaughter by negligence or random chance has ramifications (cf. 19:4). In the ancient world accidental death on one's property could trigger the retaliation of blood vengeance.

The parapet is a short wall on the edge of a roof to prevent people from falling. Ancient roofs were mostly flat and used as guest quarters, working space, and even a site for sacrifices and ritual mourning (Josh 2:6; 1 Sam 9:25-26; Jer 19:13; Zeph 1:5). The use of roof space for such purposes is still evidenced in Eastern countries and requires sturdy construction to handle the weight and foot traffic involved.

22:9-12 Combined objects

On one level these directives regarding agriculture and clothing represent an abiding respect for order in creation. The first creation account in Genesis 1 depicts order out of chaos and the human stewardship of creation as seminal values. These principles lie behind legal concerns about whatever causes or symbolically represents chaos. Hence, elements in nature that do not naturally commingle are anomalous and taboo (Lev 19:19).

A diatribe against magic may also be involved. Magic and incantations in the ancient Near East involved supernatural powers channeled and controlled by ritual activity. The concoction of unrelated ingredients in precise measurements (herbal folk medicine, potions, etc.) and verbal incantations were perceived as powerful forces. Hence, the mixing of otherwise distinct agricultural categories is suspect in Deuteronomic theology. Rabbinic Judaism picked up on these laws, elaborating and systematizing them in the Mishnah. The mention of tassels or twisted cords (v. 12) is an

Marriage Legislation. [13]If a man, after marrying a woman and having relations with her, comes to dislike her, [14]and accuses her of misconduct and slanders her by saying, "I married this woman, but when I approached her I did not find evidence of her virginity," [15]the father and mother of the young woman shall take the evidence of her virginity and bring it to the elders at the city gate. [16]There the father of the young woman shall say to the elders, "I gave my daughter to this man in marriage, but he has come to dislike her, [17]and now accuses her of misconduct, saying: 'I did not find evidence of your daughter's virginity.' But here is the evidence of my daughter's virginity!" And they shall spread out the cloth before the elders of the city. [18]Then these city elders shall take the man and discipline him, [19]and fine him one hundred silver shekels, which they shall give to the young woman's father, because the man slandered a virgin in Israel. She shall remain his wife, and he may not divorce her as long as he lives. [20]But if this charge is true, and evidence of the young woman's virginity is not found, [21]they shall bring the young woman to the entrance of her father's house and

---

item that gained prominence in rabbinic Judaism. Attitudes, behaviors, and appearances speak to covenant loyalty and serve to distinguish the community member from others around them.

22:13-29 Rules of betrothal and marriage

Marriage law in the ancient world was highly patriarchal and sensitive to human sexuality as a powerful force in nature. Pagan religions took this energy into the realm of the cult to curry favor from the gods and promote fertility in the land.

The laws here address a number of issues, that is, attraction, virginity, and alleged adultery. A husband may no longer find his bride attractive and bring the accusation of nonvirginity as a pretext for divorce. The woman's family may intervene to challenge such alleged shame upon their name. The penalty for the husband's false accusation is harsh. He must pay a fine and have no further recourse to divorce her. Should he prove to be right, she is to be stoned (v. 21; cf. 21:21). The penalty for consensual violation of another man's marriage is death for both parties. This precept illustrates the penalties for adultery as in the sixth commandment. The point about sexual assault in the city or in the open field (vv. 23-27) refers to the victim's ability to cry for help and be heard. Such mitigating circumstances are a means of protecting the powerless from falsely accused complicity. Rape of

there the men of her town shall stone her to death, because she committed a shameful crime in Israel by prostituting herself in her father's house. Thus shall you purge the evil from your midst.

²²If a man is discovered lying with a woman who is married to another, they both shall die, the man who was lying with the woman as well as the woman. Thus shall you purge the evil from Israel.

²³If there is a young woman, a virgin who is betrothed, and a man comes upon her in the city and lies with her, ²⁴you shall bring them both out to the gate of the city and there stone them to death: the young woman because she did not cry out though she was in the city, and the man because he violated his neighbor's wife. Thus shall you purge the evil from your midst. ²⁵But if it is in the open fields that a man comes upon the betrothed young woman, seizes her and lies with her, only the man who lay with her shall die. ²⁶You shall do nothing to the young woman, since the young woman is not guilty of a capital offense. As when a man rises up against his neighbor and murders him, so in this case: ²⁷it was in the open fields that he came upon her, and though the betrothed young woman may have cried out, there was no one to save her.

²⁸If a man comes upon a young woman, a virgin who is not betrothed, seizes her and lies with her, and they are discovered, ²⁹the man who lay with her shall give the young woman's father fifty silver shekels and she will be his wife, because he has violated her. He may not divorce her as long as he lives.

23 ¹A man shall not marry his father's wife, nor shall he dishonor his father's bed.

---

an unbetrothed virgin incurs a fine upon the man and disallows recourse to divorce (vv. 28-29; cf. 18-19). But for all practical purposes, the woman is treated like damaged goods.

Like other passages in Deuteronomy, this section is punctuated by the threefold repetition of purging evil from the midst of the people (vv. 21, 22, 24; cf. 19:18-19; 24:7). False witness, adultery, rape, kidnapping, and other heinous crimes impact the family and larger community. Purging sin is a communal responsibility in the land.

23:1 Incest

Although the Scriptures have no precise term for "incest," illicit familial sexual union is a taboo. Degrees of licit and illicit sexual union are not as refined as in most modern law codes, but certainly such cases as the one described here (marrying one's stepmother) are widely forbidden and are cited as so in the New Testament as well (1 Cor 5:1-5).

Membership in the Assembly. [2]No one whose testicles have been crushed or whose penis has been cut off may come into the assembly of the LORD. [3]No one born of an illicit union may come into the assembly of the LORD, nor any descendant of such even to the tenth generation may come into the assembly of the LORD. [4]No Ammonite or Moabite may ever come into the assembly of the LORD, nor may any of their descendants even to the tenth generation come into the assembly of the LORD, [5]because they would not come to meet you with food and water on your journey after you left Egypt, and because they hired Balaam, son of Beor, from Pethor in Aram Naharaim, to curse you. [6]The LORD, your God, would not listen to Balaam but turned his curse into a blessing for you, because the LORD, your God, loves you. [7]Never seek their welfare or prosperity as long as you live. [8]Do not abhor the Edomite: he is your brother. Do not abhor the Egyptian: you were a resident alien in his country. [9]Children born to them may come into the assembly of the LORD in the third generation.

23:2-9 The assembly of the Lord

The phrase "assembly of the LORD" punctuates this section (vv. 2, 3, 9). This particular Hebrew term for community (*qāhāl*) represents a variety of situations, including national identity and admission to worship. The term does not specifically include legislative or judicial contexts. Despite Deuteronomic sensitivity to the resident alien (1:16; 10:18-19), the law emphasizes what is distinctive in Israel's social and cultic life. Hence, genital mutilation is taboo. The exact reason for this exclusion is not stated but does relate to rejection of pagan fertility rites and the loss of procreation in the individual. The rejection of children born of an incestuous union relates to boundaries of blood and marriage. It also implies the rejection of children conceived in the context of fertility rites.

With the average life span in the ancient world being forty years or so, the tenth generation bespeaks a lengthy period of time. The list of nations is also informative. Ammonites and Moabites are excluded, while Edomites and Egyptians enjoy some status. Ammon and Moab are linked to alliances against Israel (Judg 3:12-14) and tied to fertility rites between gods and consorts. Moab is a traditional enemy of ancient Israel (1 Sam 14:47). In contrast, Edom is related to Esau, the brother of Jacob. Egypt, while the land of exodus, is also remembered as a place of refuge in famine or flight. Abraham and Jacob migrate to Egypt (Gen 12:10-20; 46:1-7); Judahites flee there in the wake of Babylonian encroachment (Jer 41:11-18). Israel is admonished not to abhor Egypt because its people were aliens in that land.

Cleanliness in Camp. ¹⁰When in camp during an expedition against your enemies, you shall keep yourselves from anything bad. ¹¹If one of you becomes unclean because of a nocturnal emission, he shall go outside the camp; he shall not come back into the camp. ¹²Toward evening, he shall bathe in water; then, when the sun has set, he may come back into the camp. ¹³Outside the camp you shall have a place set aside where you shall go. ¹⁴You shall keep a trowel in your equipment and, when you go outside to relieve yourself, you shall dig a hole with it and then cover up your excrement. ¹⁵Since the Lᴏʀᴅ, your God, journeys along in the midst of your camp to deliver you and to give your enemies over to you, your camp must be holy, so that he does not see anything indecent in your midst and turn away from you.

Various Precepts. ¹⁶You shall not hand over to their master any slaves who have taken refuge with you from their master. ¹⁷Let them live among you in any place they choose, in any one of your communities that seems good to them. Do not oppress them.

23:10-15 Purity during war

This law reflects rules of personal and ritual hygiene while on military duty. The depiction is not absolute, since the Lord's Tent of Meeting itself is described elsewhere as pitched outside the camp (Exod 33:7). "Outside the camp" in Deuteronomy is the place for impurity (vv. 11, 13, 14). In mind is the demand that soldiers observe a fastidious purity as they go forth in battle. The Lord goes forth with Israel's army, so its ranks must maintain holiness in the presence of the Holy. For example, Uriah the Hittite stays encamped with his troops rather than spend the night with his wife Bathsheba while back in Jerusalem (2 Sam 11:6-11). Even human bodily fluids represent impurity (Lev 15; Num 5:1-4).

23:16–25:19 Various communal precepts

These laws address aspects of personal integrity and social harmony. They are not organized systematically. The spirit herein emphasizes care of the poor and marginalized who are members of the community or enter its midst and must be welcomed. The memory of past kindness must not be forgotten, a point that echoes the Deuteronomic theology of remembering/ forgetting.

23:16-17 Slaves in flight

This precept deals with asylum for runaway slaves from foreign masters. Such refugees must be granted sanctuary at whatever place they choose. Two key issues are at work here. First, Israel must maintain its covenant

¹⁸There shall be no temple prostitute among the Israelite women, nor a temple prostitute among the Israelite men. ¹⁹You shall not offer a prostitute's fee or a dog's pay as any kind of votive offering in the house of the LORD, your God; both these things are an abomination to the LORD, your God.

²⁰You shall not demand interest from your kindred on a loan of money or of food or of anything else which is loaned. ²¹From a foreigner you may demand

---

loyalty to the Lord, remembering that its ancestors were once slaves in Egypt. Second, although the biblical evidence and historical data of the time provide no systematic and overarching provisions for extradition, ancient Near Eastern codes evidence harsh penalties for runaway slaves and those who help them. Slavery as spoils of war and as debt-bondage is the predominant scenario (15:1-18). Deuteronomy is quite unique in its protection of runaway slaves and other persons at risk. In the New Testament an example of the negotiation of slave ownership and manumission is the Letter to Philemon.

23:18-19 Cultic prostitution

This prohibition is another bald diatribe in Deuteronomy against the pagan practice of associating sexual relations with attaining divine access and favor. The power involved is tied to the energy of fertility and procreation. Further, the mention of any kind of votive offerings indicates rejection of tainted money. This detail deserves comment because it represents in every age monetary or bartered exchange for goods and services, as well as selling a person at a paltry price. The "dog's pay" (v. 19) is especially pejorative. In the Old Testament dogs are dirty scavengers that roam about and interbreed indiscriminately. To call someone a dog is deemed a vile insult (1 Sam 17:43; Ps 22:17).

23:20-21 Interest on loans

As already evident in Deuteronomy, modern standards of social order and justice do not always apply. Such is the case with making loans for profit. In the Scriptures usury among family and community members is frowned upon, while more acceptable and widespread with outsiders. This prohibition guards against the economic exploitation of the Israelite. Further, in any age uneven monetary structures involve conversion rates that can be manipulated for unfair profit (Matt 21:12). Profiting on loans smacks of exploitation, a concern in several aspects of Old Testament literature (Prov 19:17; 28:8; cf. Exod 22:24; Pss 15:5; 37:26; Ezek 18:7-8). Ideally, a loan is not opportunistic but saves another person from economic disaster.

interest, but you may not demand interest from your kindred, so that the LORD, your God, may bless you in all your undertakings on the land you are to enter and possess.

²²When you make a vow to the LORD, your God, you shall not delay in fulfilling it; for the LORD, your God, will surely require it of you and you will be held guilty. ²³Should you refrain from making a vow, you will not be held guilty. ²⁴But whatever your tongue utters you must be careful to do, just as you freely vowed to the LORD, your God, with your own mouth.

²⁵When you go through your neighbor's vineyard, you may eat as many grapes as you wish, until you are satisfied, but do not put them in your basket. ²⁶When you go through your neighbor's grainfield, you may pluck some of the ears with your hand, but do not put a sickle to your neighbor's grain.

24 Marriage Legislation. ¹When a man, after marrying a woman, is later displeased with her because he ▶

23:22-24 Keeping vows

In general a vow is a promise to perform or refrain from something that fosters personal happiness and spiritual life. Vows can be private or public. In the Old Testament vows take a variety of forms. For example, Nazirites vow to live a distinct lifestyle that sets them apart and leads them to holiness (Num 6:1-21). Individuals take vows in hope of divine favor or rescue from distress (1 Sam 1:9-11; Ps 66:14). Once made, vows must be fulfilled and are not to be trivialized. To compromise a vow brings on disaster, because such conduct breaks a promise to the Lord (v. 24; cf. Prov 20:25; Eccl 5:4).

23:25-26 Gleaning

This law speaks once more to the theology of ecology. The gifts of the earth come from the Lord and belong to all creatures. A careful balance is offered, i.e., the resident poor and the traveler are fed while the integrity of the owner's property is basically respected. The donee must not cart off what cannot be eaten along the way. A notable example of this tenet is Ruth's gleaning of the field of Boaz (Ruth 2). Such openness represents hospitality, a value in Israel and the broader Greco-Roman world as represented in tales of gods or angels disguised as travelers seeking hospitality (Gen 18:2-8; Tob 5:4; Heb 13:1). This section anticipates Deuteronomy 26 and thanksgiving for the harvest.

24:1-5 Marriage legislation

In Deuteronomy someone cannot remarry his divorced wife who subsequently marries another man. The exact nature of this law is unclear but

finds in her something indecent, and he writes out a bill of divorce and hands it to her, thus dismissing her from his house, ²if on leaving his house she goes and becomes the wife of another man, ³and the second husband, too, comes to dislike her and he writes out a bill of divorce and hands it to her, thus dismissing her from his house, or if this second man who has married her dies, ⁴then her former husband, who dismissed her, may not again take her as his wife after she has become defiled. That would be an abomination before the LORD, and you shall not bring such guilt upon the land the LORD, your God, is giving you as a heritage.

⁵When a man is newly wed, he shall not go out on a military expedition, nor shall any duty be imposed on him. He shall be exempt for one year for the sake of his family, to bring joy to the wife he has married.

Pledges and Kidnappings. ⁶No one shall take a hand mill or even its upper stone as a pledge for debt, for that would be taking as a pledge the debtor's life.

---

may represent a desire to preserve the traditional and legal boundaries of marriage, divorce, and adultery. A document of divorce allows a woman to remarry without the penalty of adultery. However, remarriage to a former spouse blurs laws regarding adultery and somehow violates another man's marriage. Jeremiah metaphorically picks up on this theme in relation to prophetic judgment on wayward Israel (Jer 3:1-5).

Exemption from military duty for the newlywed husband harks back to 20:5-8 where this point is discussed in greater detail, as well as the purity-in-the-camp laws in 23:11-12. Normal bodily functions and willful sexual activities can create ritual impurities in various ways. Further, in the ancient world tales of the perils of newlyweds and even wedding night death are noteworthy (Tob 3:7-9; 8:1-21). But on a positive note, Deuteronomy shows loving concern for those just married. To enjoy a one-year exemption from military service allows a couple to grow closer and perhaps bear a child. Military life includes the possibility of war and death, an eventuality that includes the possibility of widowhood and orphaned children.

24:6 Objects taken in pledge

Goods held in pledge should not impact on the debtor's essential needs. Given the fact that in the ancient world bread was prepared daily from the mill, such seizure disrupts family life. Hence, the millstone is unjust collateral. Metaphorically, the silence of the grinding mill represents desolation (Jer 25:10; Rev 18:21-22).

⁷If anyone is caught kidnapping a fellow Israelite, enslaving or selling the victim, that kidnapper shall be put to death. Thus shall you purge the evil from your midst.

Skin Diseases. ⁸In an attack of scaly infection you shall be careful to observe exactly and to carry out all the instructions the levitical priests give you, as I have commanded them: observe them carefully. ⁹Remember what the LORD, your God, did to Miriam on the journey after you left Egypt.

Loans and Wages. ¹⁰When you make a loan of any kind to your neighbor, you shall not enter the neighbor's house to receive the pledge, ¹¹but shall wait outside until the person to whom you are

---

24:7 Kidnapping

The matter of holding someone for ransom is probably secondary here. More to the point, selling another Israelite into slavery is an outrage and capital offense (cf. Exod 21:16). Kinship in covenant with God precludes such misconduct and is a clear violation of the Ten Commandments.

24:8-9 Skin diseases

In the ancient world this malady was not limited to the modern medical definition of Hansen's disease discovered in the nineteenth century. Any scaly infection was included and referred to the Levitical priests or other authorities for diagnosis and treatment. Laws regarding scaly infection are more fully discussed in Leviticus 13–14. Symptoms such as flakes and boils were included. Even clothing and dwellings could be condemned as infected (Lev 13:47-59; 14:34-57). Social order and canons of purity/impurity were the driving forces behind such laws, not medical expertise. Moses and Miriam are both remembered as victims of scaly infection and show, respectively, divine power and divine judgment (Exod 4:6-7; Num 12:9-15). The New Testament largely departs from the traditional shunning of persons with a scaly infection, which is a splendid metaphor for Jesus' association with sinners and other outcasts (Matt 10:8; Mark 1:41).

24:10-13 Further on pledges

Collecting debts should not be intrusive or violate the canons of honor and shame. By not entering the house, the creditor allows the debtor to have charge of whatever pledge is brought outside. The home is not violated. Whether actually an observed law or more an expression of charity, to return garments taken in pledge shows sensitivity to the poor (v. 17). Clothing

making the loan brings the pledge outside to you. ¹²If the person is poor, you shall not sleep in the pledged garment, ¹³but shall definitely return it at sunset, so that your neighbor may sleep in the garment and bless you. That will be your justice before the Lord, your God.

¹⁴You shall not exploit a poor and needy hired servant, whether one of your own kindred or one of the resident aliens who live in your land, within your gates. ¹⁵On each day you shall pay the servant's wages before the sun goes down, since the servant is poor and is counting on them. Otherwise the servant will cry to the Lord against you, and you will be held guilty.

Individual Responsibility. ¹⁶Parents shall not be put to death for their children, nor shall children be put to death for their parents; only for one's own crime shall a person be put to death.

is personal, and the poor lack the wardrobe of the wealthy. Clothing also symbolizes one's social status and must not impact the integrity of the community and its worship (Jas 2:2-3).

24:14-15 Just wages

Once again Deuteronomy shows care for the poor, whether native or resident alien. Many people live hand-to-mouth and cannot afford to lose a day's pay due to an unscrupulous employer (Lev 19:13). The prophets railed against defrauding the poor (Jer 22:13; Mal 3:5).

In ancient times employment depended on seasonal agricultural conditions, weather, and related factors. Wages were traditionally negotiated rather than regulated. Services included such tasks as midwifery, construction, farming, shepherding, and fishing.

24:16 Individual responsibility

Although seemingly contrary to the spirit of Deuteronomy 5:9, this stipulation is valid. Even though the ancient world had a larger sense of corporate personality than many moderns do, the individual held a level of personal responsibility. Read together, these verses recall the deepest tragedy of crime, i.e., the individual is responsible, but there are always ramifications for the larger community. Personal guilt and communal guilt are not mutually exclusive.

The Scriptures do not take a single position on sin and punishment. Such is the point of the proverb about eating "sour grapes" (Jer 31:29; Ezek 18:2-3). Sirach 15 complements this issue with its sage reflection on free will and the individual conscience.

Rights of the Unprotected. ¹⁷You shall not deprive the resident alien or the orphan of justice, nor take the clothing of a widow as pledge. ¹⁸For, remember, you were slaves in Egypt, and the LORD, your God, redeemed you from there; that is why I command you to do this.

¹⁹When you reap the harvest in your field and overlook a sheaf in the field, you shall not go back to get it; let it be for the resident alien, the orphan, and the widow, so that the LORD, your God, may bless you in all your undertakings. ²⁰When you knock down the fruit of your olive trees, you shall not go over the branches a second time; let what remains be for the resident alien, the orphan, and the widow. ²¹When you pick your grapes, you shall not go over the vineyard a second time; let what remains be for the resident alien, the orphan, and the widow. ²²For remember that you were slaves in the land of Egypt; that is why I command you to do this.

25 Limits on Punishments. ¹When there is a dispute and the parties draw near for judgment, and a decision is given, declaring one party in the right and the other in the wrong, ²if the one in the wrong deserves whipping, the judge shall have him lie down and in the pres-

24:17-22 The memory of Egypt

This section is delimited by the inclusion, "You were slaves in Egypt" (vv. 18, 22). This grand memory is so much a part of Israel's self-understanding. Ransom from Egypt does not involve an exchange of money (7:8; 13:6; cf. Mic 6:4). In the book of Exodus the Lord never speaks to Pharaoh, never negotiates a diplomatic compromise, and basically sets the people free at no cost. In fact, they leave Egypt with impressive spoils (Exod 3:22; 12:36). In the Israelite cult the ransom motif expresses itself in redemption of the firstborn by a sacrificial animal or monetary donation.

This theological perspective provides a motive for the prosperous in Israel to share their wealth. During the harvest allow no second harvest; let the poor glean from the leftover produce. Such virtue shows compassion to the needy and reminds the wealthy of the humble lesson that the land belongs to the Lord.

25:1-3 Human dignity and punishment

The gist of this regulation is the preservation of human dignity when punishing a convicted criminal. A maximum number of stripes sets boundaries that guard against unbridled retribution. Corporal punishment in the ancient world (and much of human history for that matter) was largely a public event intended to warn others and bring shame on the culprit's family. Corporal punishment, especially of children, is more and more

ence of the judge receive the number of lashes the crime warrants. ³Forty lashes may be given, but no more; or else, if more lashes are added to these many blows, your brother will be degraded in your sight.

Treatment of Oxen. ⁴You shall not muzzle an ox when it treads out grain.

Levirate Marriage. ⁵When brothers live together and one of them dies without a son, the widow of the deceased shall not marry anyone outside the family; but her husband's brother shall come to her, marrying her and performing the duty of a brother-in-law. ⁶The firstborn son she bears shall continue the name of the deceased brother, that his name may not be blotted out from Israel. ⁷But if a man does not want to marry his brother's wife, she shall go up to the elders at the gate and say, "My brother-in-law refuses to perpetuate his brother's name in Israel and does not intend to perform his duty toward me." ⁸Thereupon the elders of his city shall summon him and speak to him. If he persists in saying, "I do not want to marry her," ⁹his sister-in-law, in the presence of the elders, shall go up to him and strip his sandal from his foot and spit in his face, declaring, "This is how one should be treated who will not build up his brother's family!" ¹⁰And his name shall be called in Israel, "the house of the man stripped of his sandal."

questioned today but has wide biblical attestation, particularly in the wisdom literature (Prov 19:29; 26:3; Sir 30:1-13). However, one must not use the Bible to condone gross physical abuse. Such harsh laws must be read in their temporal and cultural context, not cited to rationalize abuses today. For example, the modern sentence of community service is an alternative to corporal punishment or incarceration.

25:4 Animal care

This pithy law harks back to 22:4, 6-7 and reflects the humane treatment of animals. Oxen were valuable animals in the ancient world and a status symbol. Given their size and strength, they were useful for plowing, treading grain, and other agricultural tasks. The New Testament draws on this verse to encourage the communal support of itinerant missionaries and local ministers (1 Cor 9:9; 1 Tim 5:18).

25:5-10 Levirate marriage

The word "Levirate" comes from the Latin word *levir*, "brother-in-law." This practice concerns providing an heir for a man who dies childless. The intent is to preserve the deceased person's name and inheritance via his nearest kinsman. The discussion is divided into two parts (vv. 5-6 and 7-10). The first part relates details of this arrangement and emphasizes maintaining what we call today the nuclear and extended family. Other issues

Various Precepts. [11]When two men are fighting and the wife of one intervenes to save her husband from the blows of his opponent, if she stretches out her hand and seizes the latter by his genitals, [12]you shall chop off her hand; show no pity.

[13]You shall not keep two differing weights in your bag, one heavy and the other light; [14]nor shall you keep two different ephahs in your house, one large and the other small. [15]But use a full and just weight, a full and just ephah, so that you may have a long life on the land the LORD, your God, is giving you. [16]For everyone who does these things, everyone who does what is dishonest, is an abomination to the LORD, your God.

[17]Bear in mind what Amalek did to you on the journey after you left Egypt, [18]how he surprised you along the way, weak and weary as you were, and struck

---

include keeping the widow's dowry in the family and, on a more charitable level, providing her with financial and material security. The second part concerns the kinsman's shirking of Levirate duty. In that case the widow brings her suit to the elders and, if the kinsman remains obstinate, she shames him openly. Her actions serve as a public display of her innocence and his guilt in the matter. Removing his sandal is an invasive gesture by a woman upon a man (cf. vv. 11-12). Spitting is a sign of contempt (Job 30:10; Mark 15:19). Genesis 38:8-18 recounts the death of Onan for not performing the duty of Levirate marriage.

25:11-12 Intervention

This law may seem extreme to the modern reader but is rooted in the violation of gender boundaries, a sociocultural demand in many cultures even today. The severity of the penalty emphasizes the gravity of the offense. The punitive loss of a hand, especially the right one, made the person a social outcast and left visible evidence of a serious criminal act.

25:13-16 Weights and measures

Lacking modern weights and standards, dishonesty in the marketplace was rampant in ancient times and protested by the prophets (Amos 8:5). Retail bargaining was a common if not expected practice. In Deuteronomy fair trade reflects social justice and fosters communal harmony.

25:17-19 The memory of Amalek

This diatribe against Amalek and the Amalekites (a notorious Bedouin tribe) is anachronistic. The group no longer exists by the time of Deuteronomy, so this is not a statute of current relevance. The text speaks more to the Deuteronomic theology of remembering/forgetting. Forget not your

down at the rear all those who lagged behind; he did not fear God. [19]Therefore, when the LORD, your God, gives you rest from all your enemies round about in the land which the LORD, your God, is giving you to possess as a heritage, you shall blot out the memory of Amalek from under the heavens. Do not forget!

26 Thanksgiving for the Harvest. [1]When you have come into the land which the LORD, your God, is giving you as a heritage, and have taken possession and settled in it, [2]you shall take some first fruits of the various products of the soil which you harvest from the land the LORD, your God, is giving you; put them in a basket and go to the place which the LORD, your God, will choose as the dwelling place for his name. [3]There you shall go to the priest in office at that time and say to him, "Today I acknowledge to the LORD, my God, that I have indeed come into the land which the LORD swore to our ancestors to give us." [4]The priest shall then take the basket from your hands and set it in front of the altar of the LORD, your God. [5]Then you shall declare in the presence of the LORD, your God, "My father was a refugee Aramean who went down to Egypt with a small household and lived there as a resident alien. But there he became a nation great, strong and numerous. [6]When the Egyptians maltreated and oppressed us, imposing harsh servitude upon us, [7]we cried to the LORD, the God of our ancestors, and the LORD heard our cry and saw our affliction, our toil and our oppression. [8]Then the LORD brought us out of Egypt with a strong hand and outstretched arm, with terrifying power, with signs and wonders, [9]and brought us to this place, and gave us this land, a land flowing with milk and honey.

enemies and all they did against you during the exodus. The modern reader may take a dim view of this stance. Forgiveness and healing cannot be attained when past abuses and hurts are held onto and handed down to later generations.

26:1-15 Remembrance and thanksgiving

"When . . ." serves to divide this section into two parts (vv. 1, 12). The first part relates to entering the land and offering some of the first fruits as an annual tithe. The second part concerns offering the fruits of the land in a triennial tithe. As stated earlier (14:22-29), tithes are portions set aside for sacred rites and services. Verses 1-11 highlight remembrance of past oppression, the exodus, and entrance into the Promised Land. The first fruits of the land are gifts from the Lord and thus holy. Without a symbolic ritual offering as return to the Lord, blessing on the rest of the crops is at risk. The prosperous must invite the disenfranchised and needy to their celebrations of the harvest.

83

Camel and pyramids, Cairo, Egypt

¹⁰Now, therefore, I have brought the first fruits of the products of the soil which you, LORD, have given me." You shall set them before the LORD, your God, and you shall bow down before the LORD, your God. ¹¹Then you and your household, together with the Levite and the resident aliens who live among you, shall celebrate with all these good things which the LORD, your God, has given you.

Declaration Concerning Tithes. ¹²When you have finished setting aside all the tithes of your produce in the third year, the year of the tithes, and have given them to the Levite, the resident alien, the orphan and the widow, that they may eat and be satisfied in your own communities, ¹³you shall declare before the LORD, your God, "I have purged my house of the sacred portion and I have given it to the Levite, the resident alien, the orphan and the widow, just as you have commanded me. I have not transgressed any of your commandments, nor forgotten any. ¹⁴I have not eaten any of the tithe while in mourning; I have not brought any of it while unclean; I have not offered any of it to the dead. I have thus obeyed the voice of the LORD, my God, and done just as you have commanded me. ¹⁵Look down, then, from heaven, your holy abode, and bless your people Israel and the fields you have given us, as you promised on oath to our ancestors, a land flowing with milk and honey."

The Covenant. ¹⁶This day the LORD, your God, is commanding you to observe these statutes and ordinances. Be

Verses 12-15 relate a local triennial celebration that emphasizes sharing stored foods with those most at risk. It is noteworthy that again in Deuteronomy the traditional classes of needy persons are cited (v. 12). The prayer (vv. 13-15) summarizes the spirit of this cultic law. The prayer includes three denials that distance the Israelite from what represents foreign practice, i.e., eating the tithes of a mourner, personal uncleanness in the cult, and making death offerings. The person has obeyed the voice of the Lord (v. 14, literally "listened to"), a common biblical phrase that emphasizes obedience. The prayer ends with a plea for continued blessing in the Promised Land.

26:16-19 Covenant as time of decision

This point in Moses' second address is punctuated by the threefold repetition of "this day" or "today" (vv. 16, 17, 18). Now is the opportune time to rededicate oneself to the commandments and life in covenant. The narrative is also highlighted by motifs from earlier in Deuteronomy: today is the time of decision (5:1) for Israel is the Lord's own people (7:6; 14:2). Such repetitions serve to emphasize key teachings in Deuteronomy. Finally, true religion is rewarded by divine favor and the esteem of surrounding nations (v. 19).

careful, then, to observe them with your whole heart and with your whole being. ¹⁷Today you have accepted the LORD's agreement: he will be your God, and you will walk in his ways, observe his statutes, commandments, and ordinances, and obey his voice. ¹⁸And today the LORD has accepted your agreement: you will be a people specially his own, as he promised you, you will keep all his commandments, ¹⁹and he will set you high in praise and renown and glory above all nations he has made, and you will be a people holy to the LORD, your God, as he promised.

27 **The Altar on Mount Ebal.** ¹Then Moses, with the elders of Israel, commanded the people, saying: Keep this whole commandment which I give you today. ²On the day you cross the Jordan into the land which the LORD, your God, is giving you, set up some large stones and coat them with plaster. ³Write on them, at the time you cross, all the words of this law, so that you may enter the land which the LORD, your God, is giving you, a land flowing with milk and honey, just as the LORD, the God of your ancestors, promised you. ⁴When you cross the Jordan, on Mount Ebal you

---

27:1–28:69 At the border of the land

With the people about to cross the Jordan River, the narrative reemphasizes curses and blessings. The assertions are oriented toward the future, from the day the people cross the Jordan (v. 2). Subsequent generations must learn and heed what the ancestors swore to embrace as they entered the Promised Land.

This section recalls the grand story of passing through the Sea of Reeds (Exod 13:17–15:27). Both sea and river share symbolic value in the saga of Israel. Wandering eastward, the people leave Egypt on their journey from slavery to freedom. The Promised Land is ever the destination during the symbolic forty years of wandering and murmuring. Now they turn back and journey westward across the Jordan and enter the land. Crossing water is a key geographical and intertextual link between the exodus and entrance into Canaan.

27:1-13 Crossing the Jordan

The Jordan is mentioned three times (vv. 2, 4, 11). The first citation of the river relates to the writing of the Deuteronomic laws on plastered stones, an event that is to take place immediately after the people cross over. The second citation calls for a stone altar of sacrifice on Mount Ebal (by Shechem and Mount Gerizim). The third citation juxtaposes the two mountains, Ebal and Gerizim, as staging points for the ritual announcement of curses

shall set up these stones concerning which I command you today, and coat them with plaster, ⁵and you shall build there an altar to the LORD, your God, an altar made of stones that no iron tool has touched. ⁶You shall build this altar of the LORD, your God, with unhewn stones, and shall offer on it burnt offerings to the LORD, your God. ⁷You shall also offer communion sacrifices and eat them there, rejoicing in the presence of the LORD, your God. ⁸On the stones you shall inscribe all the words of this law very clearly.

⁹Moses, with the levitical priests, then said to all Israel: Be silent, Israel, and listen! This day you have become the people of the LORD, your God. ¹⁰You shall obey the voice of the LORD, your God, and keep his commandments and statutes which I am giving you today.

Preparation for Blessings and Curses. ¹¹That same day Moses commanded the people, saying: ¹²When you cross the Jordan, these shall stand on Mount Gerizim to bless the people: Simeon, Levi, Judah, Issachar, Joseph and Benjamin. ¹³And these shall stand on Mount Ebal for the curse: Reuben, Gad, Asher, Zebulun, Dan and Naphtali.

The Twelve Curses. ¹⁴The Levites shall proclaim in a loud voice to all the Israelites: ¹⁵"Cursed be anyone who makes a carved or molten idol, an abomination to the LORD, the work of a craftsman's hands, and sets it up in secret!" And all the people shall answer, "Amen!"

---

and blessings by members of the twelve tribes. In the Bible the Jordan is a geographical locus and memorial marker for a variety of important events (Gen 50:10-11; Josh 12:1-24; Matt 3:13-17; Mark 10:1).

27:14–28:69 Curses and blessings in the land

Interspersed with other material, a litany of curses and blessings informs this section. The pronouncements are in random order and touch on a variety of topics.

27:14-26 Twelve curses

A number of Hebrew words denote a curse. The verb here (Hebrew ʿarar) has the semantic range of casting spells, banning persons or things, and the withdrawal of some strength or benefit. It is noteworthy that the element of secrecy is included in the curses (vv. 15, 24). Even when not explicitly defined as secret, a number of the curses imply stealth (e.g., vv. 17, 18, 20, 25).

In Israelite thought the power of a curse (or blessing) is rooted not in the human person but in the holiness of God and divine will. The "Amen" response to each one proclaims these laws as steadfast truths.

¹⁶"Cursed be anyone who dishonors father or mother!" And all the people shall answer, "Amen!"

¹⁷"Cursed be anyone who moves a neighbor's boundary markers!" And all the people shall answer, "Amen!"

¹⁸"Cursed be anyone who misleads the blind on their way!" And all the people shall answer, "Amen!"

¹⁹"Cursed be anyone who deprives the resident alien, the orphan or the widow of justice!" And all the people shall answer, "Amen!"

²⁰"Cursed be anyone who has relations with his father's wife, for he dishonors his father's bed!" And all the people shall answer, "Amen!"

²¹"Cursed be anyone who has relations with any animal!" And all the people shall answer, "Amen!"

²²"Cursed be anyone who has relations with his sister, whether his father's daughter or his mother's daughter!" And all the people shall answer, "Amen!"

²³"Cursed be anyone who has relations with his mother-in-law!" And all the people shall answer, "Amen!"

²⁴"Cursed be anyone who strikes down a neighbor in secret!" And all the people shall answer, "Amen!"

²⁵"Cursed be anyone who accepts payment to kill an innocent person!" And all the people shall answer, "Amen!"

²⁶"Cursed be anyone whose actions do not uphold the words of this law!" And all the people shall answer, "Amen!"

28 **Blessings for Obedience.** ¹Now, if you diligently obey the voice of the LORD, your God, carefully observing all his commandments which I give you today, the LORD, your God, will set you high above all the nations of the earth. ²All these blessings will come upon you and overwhelm you when you obey the voice of the LORD, your God:

³May you be blessed in the city,
and blessed in the country!
⁴Blessed be the fruit of your womb,
the produce of your soil and the
offspring of your livestock,
the issue of your herds and the
young of your flocks!
⁵Blessed be your grain basket and
your kneading bowl!
⁶May you be blessed in your coming in,
and blessed in your going out!

Victory and Prosperity. ⁷The LORD will beat down before you the enemies that rise up against you; they will come out against you from one direction, and flee before you in seven. ⁸The LORD will affirm the blessing upon you, on your barns and on all your undertakings; he will bless you in the land that the LORD,

---

28:1-14 A pattern of blessings

Blessing brings prosperity and is connected to hearing the Lord's voice (vv. 1, 2; cf. v. 15 on curse). These blessings are artfully presented in a merism, a figure of speech that cites extremes but presumes everything between them (e.g., high and low, young and old). Blessing is caught up in fertility of

your God, is giving you. ⁹The LORD will establish you as a holy people, as he swore to you, if you keep the commandments of the LORD, your God, and walk in his ways. ¹⁰All the peoples of the earth will see that the name of the LORD is proclaimed over you, and they will be afraid of you. ¹¹The LORD will generously increase the fruit of your womb, the offspring of your livestock, and the produce of your soil, upon the land which the LORD swore to your ancestors he would give you. ¹²The LORD will open up for you his rich storehouse, the heavens, to give your land rain in due season and to bless all the works of your hands. You will lend to many nations but borrow from none. ¹³The LORD will make you the head not the tail, the top not the bottom, if you obey the commandments of the LORD, your God, which I am giving you today, observing them carefully, ¹⁴not turning aside, either to the right or to the left, from any of the words which I am giving you today, following other gods and serving them.

Curses for Disobedience. ¹⁵But if you do not obey the voice of the LORD, your God, carefully observing all his commandments and statutes which I give you today, all these curses shall come upon you and overwhelm you:

¹⁶May you be cursed in the city, and cursed in the country! ¹⁷Cursed be your grain basket and your kneading bowl! ¹⁸Cursed be the fruit of your womb, the produce of your soil and the offspring of your livestock, the issue of your herds

the soil and the womb, bringing forth plant and animal life in all its forms. However, in ancient thought plants were deemed not to be alive because they did not move about. Verses 7-14 elaborate on some specific benefits of blessing: victory over the enemy and international renown. These favors are contingent on keeping the Deuteronomic laws (v. 9). Ideally, divine blessing is associated with peace among the nations, despite the pervasive presence of war in the Old Testament.

Picking up from 11:10-17, rain nourishes the land in due season (v. 12). In the Scriptures the Lord is the one who causes rain and the one who makes possible life and happiness in the Promised Land (Deut 11:10-17; cf. Job 28:26; Jer 14:22).

28:15-69 Curses for disobedience

This lengthy section begins with another series of curses (vv. 16-19) that contrast with the blessings cited above. Moses' second address ends on a negative note but also serves as a firm exhortation to obedience. Although not outright apocalyptic, the language borders on this genre as depicted in the book of Revelation.

and the young of your flocks! [19]May you be cursed in your coming in, and cursed in your going out!

Sickness and Defeat. [20]The LORD will send on you a curse, panic, and frustration in everything you set your hand to, until you are speedily destroyed and perish for the evil you have done in forsaking me. [21]The LORD will make disease cling to you until he has made an end of you from the land you are entering to possess. [22]The LORD will strike you with consumption, fever, and inflammation, with fiery heat and drought, with blight and mildew, that will pursue you until you perish. [23]The heavens over your heads will be like bronze and the earth under your feet like iron. [24]For rain the LORD will give your land powdery dust, which will come down upon you from the heavens until you are destroyed. [25]The LORD will let you be beaten down before your enemies; though you advance against them from one direction, you will flee before them in seven, so that you will become an object of horror to all the kingdoms of the earth. [26]Your corpses will become food for all the birds of the air and for the beasts of the field, with no one to frighten them off. [27]The LORD will strike you with Egyptian boils and with tumors, skin diseases and the itch, from none of which you can be cured. [28]And the LORD will strike you with madness, blindness and panic, [29]so that even at midday you will grope in the dark as though blind, unable to find your way.

Despoilment. You will be oppressed and robbed continually, with no one to come to your aid. [30]Though you betroth a wife, another will have her. Though you build a house, you will not live in it. Though you plant a vineyard, you will not pluck its fruits. [31]Your ox will be slaughtered before your eyes, but you will not eat its flesh. Your donkey will be stolen in your presence, but you will never get it back. Your flocks will be given to your enemies, with no one to come to your aid. [32]Your sons and daughters will be given to another people while you strain your eyes looking for them every day, having no power to do anything. [33]A people you do not know will consume the fruit of your soil and of all your labor, and you will be thoroughly oppressed and continually crushed, [34]until you are driven mad by what your eyes must look upon. [35]The LORD will strike you with malignant boils of which you cannot be cured, on your knees and legs, and from the soles of your feet to the crown of your head.

Exile. [36]The LORD will bring you, and your king whom you have set over you, to a nation which you and your ancestors have not known, and there you will serve other gods, of wood and stone, [37]and you will be a horror, a byword, a

---

Among the overarching themes and motifs depicted here, several are notable. First, the repetition of the voice of the Lord (vv. 15, 45) and rain (v. 24) stitch the narrative to the motif of blessing discussed above. Second, the horrific physical afflictions and other disasters recall the plagues in Exodus 7–11 and the more historically proximate sieges of Jerusalem

taunt among all the peoples to which the LORD will drive you.

Fruitless Labors. ³⁸Though you take out seed to your field, you will harvest but little, for the locusts will devour it. ³⁹Though you plant and cultivate vineyards, you will not drink or store up the wine, for the worms will eat them. ⁴⁰Though you have olive trees throughout your country, you will have no oil for ointment, for your olives will drop off. ⁴¹Though you beget sons and daughters, they will not remain with you, for they will go into captivity. ⁴²Buzzing insects will take possession of all your trees and the crops of your soil. ⁴³The resident aliens among you will rise above you higher and higher, while you sink lower and lower. ⁴⁴They will lend to you, not you to them. They will become the head, you the tail.

⁴⁵All these curses will come upon you, pursuing you and overwhelming you, until you are destroyed, because you would not obey the voice of the LORD, your God, by keeping his commandments and statutes which he gave you. ⁴⁶They will be a sign and a wonder for you and your descendants for all time. ⁴⁷Since you would not serve the LORD, your God, with heartfelt joy for abundance of every kind, ⁴⁸in hunger and thirst, in nakedness and utter want, you will serve the enemies whom the LORD will send against you. He will put an iron yoke on your neck, until he destroys you.

Invasion and Siege. ⁴⁹The LORD will raise up against you a nation from afar, from the end of the earth, that swoops down like an eagle, a nation whose language you do not understand, ⁵⁰a nation of fierce appearance, that shows neither respect for the aged nor mercy for the young. ⁵¹They will consume the offspring of your livestock and the produce of your soil, until you are destroyed; they will leave you no grain or wine or oil, no issue of herd, no young of flock, until they have brought about your ruin. ⁵²They will besiege you in each of your communities, until the great, fortified walls, in which you trust, come tumbling down all over your land. They will besiege you in every community throughout the land which the LORD, your God, has given you, ⁵³and because of the siege and the distress to which your enemy subjects you, you will eat the fruit of your womb, the flesh of your own sons and daughters whom the LORD, your God, has given you. ⁵⁴The most refined and fastidious man among you will begrudge his brother and his beloved wife and his surviving children, ⁵⁵any share in the flesh of his children that he himself is using for food because nothing else is left him—such the siege and dis-

---

(597–587 B.C.) surrounding the Babylonian exile. Third, oppression connotes speaking falsely of or doing wrong to another, especially by extortion (Lev 19:11; Ps 146:7). Fourth, exile and indentured service are symbolized by the yoke (v. 48), a fitting motif for oppression as a consequence of sin. However, in the Scriptures the yoke also has a positive meaning when one hears the voice of the Lord and lives rightly (Sir 6:24-26; Matt 11:28-30).

tress to which your enemy will subject you in all your communities. [56]The most fastidious woman among you, who would not venture to set the sole of her foot on the ground, so refined and fastidious is she, will begrudge her beloved husband and her son and daughter [57]the afterbirth that issues from her womb and the infants she brings forth because she secretly eats them for want of anything else—such the siege and distress to which your enemy will subject you in your communities.

Plagues. [58]If you are not careful to observe all the words of this law which is written in this book, and to fear this glorious and awesome name, the LORD, your God, [59]the LORD will bring upon you and your descendants wondrous calamities, severe and constant calamities, and malignant and constant sicknesses. [60]He will bring back upon you all the diseases of Egypt which you dread, and they will cling to you. [61]Even any sickness or calamity not written in this book of the law, that too the LORD will bring upon you until you are destroyed. [62]You who were numerous as the stars of the heavens will be left few in number, because you would not obey the voice of the LORD, your God.

Exile. [63]Just as the LORD once took delight in making you prosper and grow, so will the LORD now take delight in ruining and destroying you, and you will be plucked out of the land you are now entering to possess. [64]The LORD will scatter you among all the peoples from one end of the earth to the other, and there you will serve other gods, of wood and stone, which you and your ancestors have not known. [65]Among these nations you will find no rest, not even a resting place for the sole of your foot, for there the LORD will give you an anguished heart and wearied eyes and a trembling spirit. [66]Your life will hang in suspense and you will stand in dread both day and night, never sure of your life. [67]In the morning you will say, "Would that it were evening!" and in the evening you will say, "Would that it were morning!" because of the dread that your heart must feel and the sight that your eyes must see. [68]The LORD will send you back in ships to Egypt, by a route which I told you that you would never see again; and there you will offer yourselves for sale to your enemies as male and female slaves, but there will be no buyer.

[69]These are the words of the covenant which the LORD commanded Moses to

---

MOSES' THIRD ADDRESS

Deuteronomy 29:1–32:52

This address is informed by the theme of time, i.e., past favors from the Lord, the current exhortation to fidelity, and what lies in the future. In sum, the speech is sweeping and comprehensive in scope. The gist of the address is a call to decision: "See, I have today set before you life and good, death and evil . . . Choose life . . ." (30:15-19).

make with the Israelites in the land of Moab, in addition to the covenant he made with them at Horeb.

III: Third Address

29 **Past Favors Recalled.** ¹Moses summoned all Israel and said to them, You have seen with your own eyes all that the Lord did in the land of Egypt to Pharaoh and all his servants and to all his land, ²the great testings your own eyes have seen, and those great signs and wonders. ³But the Lord has not given you a heart to understand, or eyes to see, or ears to hear until this day. ⁴I led you for forty years in the wilderness. Your clothes did not fall from you in tatters nor your sandals from your feet; ⁵it was not bread that you ate, nor wine or beer that you drank—so that you might know that I, the Lord, am your God. ⁶When you came to this place, Sihon, king of Heshbon, and Og, king of Bashan, came out to engage us in battle, but we defeated them ⁷and took their land, and gave it as a heritage to the Reubenites, Gadites, and the half-tribe of Manasseh. ⁸Observe carefully the words of this covenant, therefore, in order that you may succeed in whatever you do.

All Israel Bound by Covenant. ⁹You are standing today, all of you, in the

---

29:1-8 Remembering the past

This brief section repeats elements of Israel's saga noted already, namely, Egyptian exile and exodus, wandering in the wilderness, and conquest of the Promised Land. Divine care is remembered as a constant on the journey. The mention of clothing in verses 4-5 reminds the reader of the Lord's tender care in spite of sin. Adam and Eve exit Eden not dressed in fig leaves but dressed by the Lord in durable leather garments (Gen 3:21); Cain is marked against random human retribution (Gen 4:15). Later, in the long wilderness experience, Israel's needs are met through divine power (Exod 16–17).

All these blessings inform the people's knowledge of God who manifests divine will in promise, election, covenant, and law. Deuteronomy echoes that Israel comes to know the Lord in the course of remembering and retelling (Exod 7:17; 11:7).

29:9-14 Assembling in the present

Deuteronomy again emphasizes Israel's covenant relationship. Here the people stand before the Lord and renew their obligations. To stand (v. 9; literally, "take one's stand") bespeaks a certain purposefulness, being appointed to fulfill a duty. The people must take courage, for the Lord goes forth with them and is ever present to them, even when the Lord is seemingly hidden or absent.

presence of the Lord, your God—your tribal heads, elders, and officials, all of the men of Israel, [10]your children, your wives, and the resident alien who lives in your camp, from those who cut wood to those who draw water for you—[11]to enter into the covenant of the Lord, your God, which the Lord, your God, is making with you today, with its curse, [12]so that he may establish you today as his people and he may be your God, as he promised you and as he swore to your ancestors, to Abraham, Isaac and Jacob. [13]But it is not with you alone that I am making this covenant, with its curse, [14]but with those who are standing here with us today in the presence of the Lord, our God, and with those who are not here with us today.

Warning Against Idolatry. [15]You know that we lived in the land of Egypt and that we passed through the nations, that you too passed through [16]and saw the loathsome things and idols of wood and stone, of gold and silver, that they possess. [17]There may be among you a man or woman, or a clan or tribe, whose heart is now turning away from the Lord, our God, to go and serve the gods of these nations; there may be among you a root bearing poison and wormwood; [18]if any such persons, after hearing the words of this curse, should congratulate themselves, saying in their hearts, "I am safe, even though I walk in stubbornness of heart," thereby sweeping away moist and dry alike, [19]the Lord will never consent to pardon them. Instead, the Lord's burning wrath will flare up against them; every curse written in this book will pounce on them, and the Lord will blot out their names from under the heavens. [20]The Lord will single them out from all the tribes of Israel for doom, in keeping with all the curses of the covenant written in this book of the law.

Punishment for Idolatry. [21]Future generations, your descendants who will

---

29:15–30:20 Fidelity in the future

As the book of Deuteronomy draws to a close, future generations are emphasized (29:21). In Hebrew a generation (*dôr*; literally, "circle") spans about forty years. Covenant abides through the cycle of life, beginning with the ancestor Abraham (Gen 17:7) and later figures. Hence, the covenant people must shun idolatry and other forms of syncretism. The explicit command against idols of wood and stone (29:16; cf. 7:5, 25) sets Israel apart from its neighbors. The theological diatribe behind this law is more than simply the fashioning of religious objects. In the ancient world gods were deemed somehow present within the figure and experienced that object's fate. Hence, statues, divination figurines, etc., could be kidnapped (Gen 31:19-35) and people actually harmed in the object's destruction (1 Sam 5:1-5). Even though early Israelite tradition acknowledged the existence of other gods, later tradition took a firmer stance that satirized pagan iconography (Ps 115:4-8).

rise up after you, as well as the foreigners who will come here from distant lands, when they see the calamities of this land and the ills the LORD has inflicted upon it—²²all its soil burned out by sulphur and salt, unsown and unfruitful, without a blade of grass, like the catastrophe of Sodom and Gomorrah, Admah and Zeboiim, which the LORD overthrew in his furious wrath—²³they and all the nations will ask, "Why has the LORD dealt thus with this land? Why this great outburst of wrath?" ²⁴And they will say, "Because they abandoned the covenant of the LORD, the God of their ancestors, which he had made with them when he brought them out of the land of Egypt, ²⁵and they went and served other gods and bowed down to them, gods whom they did not know and whom he had not apportioned to them. ²⁶So the anger of the LORD flared up against this land and brought on it every curse written in this book. ²⁷The LORD uprooted them from their soil in anger, fury, and great wrath, and cast them out into another land, as they are today." ²⁸The hidden things belong to the LORD our God, but the revealed things are for us and for our children forever, to observe all the words of this law.

30 Compassion for the Repentant.

¹When all these things, the blessing and the curse which I have set before you, come upon you, and you take them to heart in any of the nations where the LORD, your God, has dispersed you, ²and return to the LORD, your God, obeying his voice, according to all that I am commanding you today, you and your children, with your whole heart and your whole being, ³the LORD, your God, will restore your fortunes and will have compassion on you; he will again gather you from all the peoples where the LORD, your God, has scattered you. ⁴Though you may have been dispersed to the farthest corner of the heavens, even from there will the LORD, your God, gather you; even from there will he bring you back. ⁵The LORD, your God, will then bring you into the land your ancestors once possessed, that you may possess it; and he will make you more prosperous and numerous than your ancestors. ⁶The LORD, your God, will circumcise your

---

Coming generations must not become complacent in the land. Divine wrath is powerful and effective (29:22, 27). Most references to anger in the Old Testament have God as the subject and God's responding to Israel's sinning. Yet, divine wrath is balanced by divine love (Exod 34:6-7; Ps 103:8-10).

The allusions to dispersion, scattering, and return refer to exile (30:1-7). Rhetorically, Israel is asked, "What have you learned? What will you do now in light of experience?" God's great act of love in renewal is circumcising their hearts (30:6). The physical act of circumcision distinguishes Israel from its neighbors, but inner disposition is equally important. As noted earlier, a positive change of heart is behind this metaphor and echoed elsewhere in the Scriptures (10:16; Jer 4:4; 9:25; cf. Rom 2:29).

hearts and the hearts of your descendants, so that you will love the LORD, your God, with your whole heart and your whole being, in order that you may live. [7]The LORD, your God, will put all those curses on your enemies and the foes who pursued you. [8]You, however, shall again obey the voice of the LORD and observe all his commandments which I am giving you today. [9]Then the LORD, your God, will generously increase your undertakings, the fruit of your womb, the offspring of your livestock, and the produce of your soil; for the LORD, your God, will again take delight in your prosperity, just as he took delight in your ancestors', [10]because you will obey the voice of the LORD, your God, keeping the commandments and statutes that are written in this book of the law, when you return to the LORD, your God, with your whole heart and your whole being.

[11]For this command which I am giving you today is not too wondrous or remote for you. [12]It is not in the heavens, that you should say, "Who will go up to the heavens to get it for us and tell us of it, that we may do it?" [13]Nor is it across the sea, that you should say, "Who will cross the sea to get it for us and tell us of it, that we may do it?" [14]No, it is something very near to you, in your mouth and in your heart, to do it.

The Choice Before Israel. [15]See, I have today set before you life and good, death and evil. [16]If you obey the commandments of the LORD, your God, which I am giving you today, loving the LORD, your God, and walking in his ways, and keeping his commandments, statutes and ordinances, you will live and grow numerous, and the LORD, your God, will bless you in the land you are entering to possess. [17]If, however, your heart turns away and you do not obey, but are led astray and bow down to other gods and serve them, [18]I tell you today that you will certainly perish; you will not have a long life on the land which you are crossing the Jordan to enter and possess. [19]I call heaven and earth today to witness against you: I have set before you life and death, the

---

Now Deuteronomy reaches its climax in a moment of decision. Israel must choose life (30:19). In doing so the people must keep the commandments for blessings in the land. Decision is highlighted by extremes, i.e., life and prosperity or death and doom. Moses' call to heaven and earth as witnesses (30:19; cf. 21:1) reflects an element in ancient Near Eastern treaties. Powerful and potentially violent forces in creation will mete out retributive justice on the noncompliant party.

The exhortation emphasizes that choice is a demand for every generation, not simply a perfunctory covenant renewal ceremony recounting the past and answered by lip service. In this regard, it is noteworthy that the people do not audibly respond to Moses' speech here. "Choice" remains a perennial question and awaited response. This pattern contrasts with the collective response of "Amen" to curses and blessings (e.g., 27:14-26).

blessing and the curse. Choose life, then, that you and your descendants may live, [20]by loving the LORD, your God, obeying his voice, and holding fast to him. For that will mean life for you, a long life for you to live on the land which the LORD swore to your ancestors, to Abraham, Isaac, and Jacob, to give to them.

31 **The Lord's Leadership.** [1]When Moses had finished speaking these words to all Israel, [2]he said to them, I am now one hundred and twenty years old and am no longer able to go out and come in; besides, the LORD has said to me, Do not cross this Jordan. [3]It is the LORD, your God, who will cross before you; he will destroy these nations before you, that you may dispossess them. (It is Joshua who will cross before you, as

the LORD promised.) [4]The LORD will deal with them just as he dealt with Sihon and Og, the kings of the Amorites, and with their country, when he destroyed them. [5]When, therefore, the LORD delivers them up to you, you shall deal with them according to the whole commandment which I have given you. [6]Be strong and steadfast; have no fear or dread of them, for it is the LORD, your God, who marches with you; he will never fail you or forsake you.

Call of Joshua. [7]Then Moses summoned Joshua and in the presence of all Israel said to him, "Be strong and steadfast, for you shall bring this people into the land which the LORD swore to their ancestors he would give them; it is you who will give them possession of it. [8]It

---

31:1–32:52 The legacy of Moses

Now the death of Moses begins to unfold. There is a sense of peace and security amid the impending turn of events. Whatever happens, the Lord marches with the Israelites and will never forsake them (20:3-4; 31:6). Joshua is commissioned to lead the conquest and tribal allotment of Canaan. He is greatly revered in later Old Testament literature (Sir 46:1-7).

Between Joshua's call and commission, a reading of the law is mandated before the full assembly (31:9-13). This is a grand and broadly inclusive liturgical event. A key admonition is, once again, to teach the law to their children lest its memory and observance be lost.

As Moses prepares the people for an orchestrated transfer of leadership to Joshua, the narrative is highlighted by references to "that time" (literally, "that day," 31:17 [2x], 18; cf. v. 21). Verses 17-18 say that divine wrath is an appropriate response to the people's disobedience, which has already occurred and is to be expected in the future. At the same time, all is right at this sacred moment. The Lord remains present to the people (Exod 3:12).

32:1-43 The Song of Moses

This song has a juridical color, akin to the ancient *rîb* or covenant lawsuit leveled by the Lord against Israel. The *rîb* is a basic form of prophetic speech

is the LORD who goes before you; he will be with you and will never fail you or forsake you. So do not fear or be dismayed."

The Reading of the Law. ⁹When Moses had written down this law, he gave it to the levitical priests who carry the ark of the covenant of the LORD, and to all the elders of Israel. ¹⁰Moses commanded them, saying, On the feast of Booths, at the prescribed time in the year for remission which comes at the end of every seven-year period, ¹¹when all Israel goes to appear before the LORD, your God, in the place which he will choose, you shall read this law aloud in the presence of all Israel. ¹²Assemble the people—men, women and children, as well as the resident aliens who live in your communities—that they may hear and so learn to fear the LORD, your God, and to observe carefully all the words of this law. ¹³Their children also, who do not know it yet, shall hear and learn to fear the LORD, your God, as long as you live on the land which you are about to cross the Jordan to possess.

Commission to Joshua. ¹⁴The LORD said to Moses, The time is now approaching for you to die. Summon Joshua, and present yourselves at the tent of meeting that I may commission him. So Moses and Joshua went and presented themselves at the tent of meeting. ¹⁵And the LORD appeared at the tent in a column of cloud; the column of cloud stood at the entrance of the tent.

A Command to Moses. ¹⁶The LORD said to Moses, Soon you will be at rest with your ancestors, and then this people will prostitute themselves by following the foreign gods among whom they will live in the land they are about to enter. They will forsake me and break the covenant which I have made with them. ¹⁷At that time my anger will flare up against them; I will forsake them and hide my face from them; they will become a prey to be devoured, and much evil and distress will befall them. At that time they will indeed say, "Is it not because our God is not in our midst that these evils have befallen us?" ¹⁸Yet I will surely hide my face at that time because of all the evil they have done in turning to other gods. ¹⁹Now, write out this song for yourselves. Teach it to the Israelites and have them recite it, so that this song may be a witness for me against the Israelites. ²⁰For when I have brought them into the land flowing with milk and honey which I promised on oath to their ancestors, and they have eaten and are satisfied and have grown fat, if they turn to other gods and serve them, despising me and breaking my covenant,

---

(Mic 6:1-8). Heaven and earth are called as witnesses, and the disobedience of the people is contrasted to the fidelity of the Lord. Israel is accused, "Yet his degenerate children have treated him basely . . ." (v. 5), and called to remembrance, "Remember the days of old . . ." (v. 7). Divine loyalty is expressed in rich poetic imagery that echoes other biblical passages. God protects Israel on the wilderness journey, metaphorically spreads wings like an eagle (Exod 19:4), and blesses them with gifts from the earth.

²¹then, when great evil and distress befall them, this song will speak to them as a witness, for it will not be forgotten if their descendants recite it. For I know what they are inclined to do even at the present time, before I have brought them into the land which I promised on oath. ²²So Moses wrote this song that same day, and he taught it to the Israelites.

Commission of Joshua. ²³Then he commissioned Joshua, son of Nun, and said to him, Be strong and steadfast, for it is you who will bring the Israelites into the land which I promised them on oath. I myself will be with you.

◄ **The Law Placed in the Ark.** ²⁴When Moses had finished writing out on a scroll the words of this law in their entirety, ²⁵Moses gave the Levites who carry the ark of the covenant of the LORD this order: ²⁶Take this book of the law and put it beside the ark of the covenant of the LORD, your God, that there it may be a witness against you. ²⁷For I already know how rebellious and stiff-necked you will be. Why, even now, while I am alive among you, you have been rebels against the LORD! How much more, then, after I am dead! ²⁸Assemble all your tribal elders and your officials before me, that I may speak these words for them to hear and so may call heaven and earth to witness against them. ²⁹For I know that after my death you are sure to act corruptly and to turn aside from the way

along which I commanded you, so that evil will befall you in time to come because you have done what is evil in the LORD's sight, and provoked him by your deeds.

The Song of Moses. ³⁰Then Moses recited the words of this song in their entirety, for the whole assembly of Israel to hear:

32 ¹Give ear, O heavens, and let me speak;
> let the earth hear the words of
> > my mouth!
²May my teaching soak in like the
> > rain,
> and my utterance drench like
> > the dew,
Like a downpour upon the grass,
> like a shower upon the crops.
³For I will proclaim the name of the
> LORD,
> praise the greatness of our God!

⁴The Rock—how faultless are his
> deeds,
> how right all his ways!
A faithful God, without deceit,
> just and upright is he!

⁵Yet his degenerate children have
> treated him basely,
> a twisted and crooked genera-
> > tion!
⁶Is this how you repay the LORD,
> so foolish and unwise a people?
Is he not your father who begot you,
> the one who made and estab-
> > lished you?

The song is artfully informed by the eightfold repetition of "rock" (vv. 4, 13, 15, 18, 30, 31[2x], 37). This motif is often a title of God and here emphasizes the Lord's faultless deeds, divine sustenance in the wilderness, and incomparability before the gods. Rock, a hard element sometimes an instrument of violence, is balanced by its association with a softer motherly

Ancient Egyptian bas relief carving

⁷Remember the days of old,
    consider the years of generations
        past.
Ask your father, he will inform you,
    your elders, they will tell you:
⁸When the Most High allotted each
        nation its heritage,
    when he separated out human
        beings,
He set up the boundaries of the
        peoples
    after the number of the divine
        beings;
⁹But the LORD's portion was his
        people;
    his allotted share was Jacob.

¹⁰He found them in a wilderness,
    a wasteland of howling desert.
He shielded them, cared for them,
    guarded them as the apple of
        his eye.
¹¹As an eagle incites its nestlings,
    hovering over its young,
So he spread his wings, took them,
    bore them upon his pinions.
¹²The LORD alone guided them,
    no foreign god was with them.

¹³He had them mount the summits
        of the land,
    fed them the produce of its
        fields;
He suckled them with honey from
        the crags
    and olive oil from the flinty rock;
¹⁴Butter from cows and milk from
        sheep,
    with the best of lambs;

Bashan bulls and goats,
    with the cream of finest wheat;
    and the foaming blood of grapes
        you drank.

¹⁵So Jacob ate and was satisfied,
    Jeshurun grew fat and kicked;
    you became fat and gross and
        gorged.
They forsook the God who made
        them
    and scorned the Rock of their
        salvation.
¹⁶With strange gods they incited
        him,
    with abominations provoked
        him to anger.
¹⁷They sacrificed to demons, to
        "no-gods,"
    to gods they had never known,
Newcomers from afar,
    before whom your ancestors
        had never trembled.
¹⁸You were unmindful of the Rock
        that begot you,
    you forgot the God who gave
        you birth.

¹⁹The LORD saw and was filled with
        loathing,
    provoked by his sons and
        daughters.
²⁰He said, I will hide my face from
        them,
    and see what becomes of them.
For they are a fickle generation,
    children with no loyalty in them!
²¹Since they have incited me with a
        "no-god,"

---

imagery, "the Rock that begot you" (32:18; cf. Ps 18). The reference to God as "father" is rare in the Old Testament (v. 6; cf. Ps 103:13; Prov 3:12).

Moses gets to view the Promised Land from across the Jordan before his death (32:48-52; cf. Num 27:12-14). This moment is full of pathos. After his great legacy— the call and commission at the burning bush, confrontation

and provoked me with their
empty idols,
I will incite them with a "no-people";
with a foolish nation I will provoke them.
²²For by my wrath a fire is kindled
that has raged to the depths of
Sheol,
It has consumed the earth with its
yield,
and set on fire the foundations
of the mountains.
²³I will heap evils upon them
and exhaust all my arrows
against them:
²⁴Emaciating hunger and consuming
fever
and bitter pestilence,
And the teeth of wild beasts I will
send among them,
with the venom of reptiles glid-
ing in the dust.
²⁵Out in the street the sword shall
bereave,
and at home the terror
For the young man and the young
woman alike,
the nursing babe as well as the
gray beard.
²⁶I said: I will make an end of them
and blot out their name from
human memory,
²⁷Had I not feared the provocation
by the enemy,
that their foes might misunder-
stand,
And say, "Our own hand won the
victory;

the LORD had nothing to do with
any of it."
²⁸For they are a nation devoid of
reason,
having no understanding.
²⁹If they had insight they would
realize this,
they would understand their end:
³⁰"How could one rout a thousand,
or two put ten thousand to
flight,
Unless it was because their Rock
sold them,
the LORD delivered them up?"

³¹Indeed, their "rock" is not like our
Rock;
our enemies are fools.
³²For their vine is from the vine of
Sodom,
from the vineyards of Gomorrah.
Their grapes are grapes of poison,
and their clusters are bitter.
³³Their wine is the venom of
serpents,
the cruel poison of vipers.
³⁴Is not this stored up with me,
sealed up in my storehouses?
³⁵Vengeance is mine and recom-
pense,
for the time they lose their foot-
ing;
Because the day of their disaster is
at hand
and their doom is rushing upon
them!

³⁶Surely, the LORD will do justice for
his people;

---

with Pharaoh, leading a murmuring people through the Red Sea and during the wilderness experience—Moses never enters Canaan. Divine freedom remains a mystery amid justice and mercy.

Moses' death outside the land is punishment for disobedience in the priestly (P) tradition; in the Deuteronomic (D) tradition Moses dies by

on his servants he will have pity.
When he sees their strength is gone,
and neither bond nor free is left,
³⁷He will say, Where are their gods,
the rock in whom they took
refuge,
³⁸Who ate the fat of their sacrifices
and drank the wine of their libations?
Let them rise up now and help you!
Let them be your protection!
³⁹See now that I, I alone, am he,
and there is no god besides me.
It is I who bring both death and life,
I who inflict wounds and heal
them,
and from my hand no one can
deliver.
⁴⁰For I raise my hand to the heavens
and will say: As surely as I live
forever,
⁴¹When I sharpen my flashing
sword,
and my hand lays hold of judgment,
With vengeance I will repay my foes
and requite those who hate me.
⁴²I will make my arrows drunk with
blood,
and my sword shall devour
flesh—
With the blood of the slain and the
captured,
from the long-haired heads of
the enemy.

⁴³Exult with him, you heavens,
bow to him, all you divine
beings!

For he will avenge the blood of his
servants,
take vengeance on his foes;
He will requite those who hate him,
and purge his people's land.

⁴⁴So Moses, together with Hoshea, son
of Nun, went and spoke all the words of
this song in the hearing of the people.

Final Appeal. ⁴⁵When Moses had finished speaking all these words to all
Israel, ⁴⁶he said to them, Take to heart all
the words that I am giving in witness
against you today, words you should
command your children, that they may
observe carefully every word of this law.
⁴⁷For this is no trivial matter for you, but
rather your very life; by this word you
will enjoy a long life on the land you are
crossing the Jordan to possess.

Moses Looks upon Canaan. ⁴⁸On
that very day the LORD said to Moses,
⁴⁹Ascend this mountain of the Abarim,
Mount Nebo in the land of Moab facing
Jericho, and view the land of Canaan,
which I am giving to the Israelites as a
possession. ⁵⁰Then you shall die on the
mountain you are about to ascend, and
shall be gathered to your people, just as
your brother Aaron died on Mount Hor
and there was gathered to his people,
⁵¹because both of you broke faith with
me among the Israelites at the waters of
Meribath-kadesh in the wilderness of
Zin: you did not manifest my holiness
among the Israelites. ⁵²You may indeed

---

taking on the sins of the people (1:37-38; 3:23-29). His burial is recorded
as on Mount Nebo. The name Nebo is often associated with a Semitic root
for height and geographically located at a site some 2,700 feet above sea
level. Such a vantage point offers a spectacular and panoramic view of the
Promised Land.

see the land from a distance, but you shall not enter that land which I am giving to the Israelites.

33 **Blessing upon the Tribes.** ¹This is the blessing with which Moses, the man of God, blessed the Israelites before he died.

²He said:

The LORD came from Sinai
  and dawned on his people from
    Seir;
  he shone forth from Mount
    Paran.
With him were myriads of holy ones;
  at his right hand advanced the
    gods.
³Indeed, lover of the peoples,
  all the holy ones are at your side;
They follow at your heels,
  carry out your decisions.
⁴Moses charged us with the law,
  as a possession for the assembly
    of Jacob.
⁵A king arose in Jeshurun
  when the chiefs of the people
    assembled,
  and the tribes of Israel united.

⁶May Reuben live and not die out,
  but let his numbers be few.

⁷Of Judah he said this:

Hear, LORD, the voice of Judah,
  and bring him to his people.
His own hands defend his cause;
  be a help against his foes.

⁸Of Levi he said:

Give to Levi your Thummim,
  your Urim to your faithful one;
Him you tested at Massah,
  contended against him at the
    waters of Meribah.
⁹He said of his father and mother,
  "I have no regard for them";
His brothers he would not acknowl-
    edge,
  and his own children he did not
    recognize.
For they kept your words,
  and your covenant they upheld.
¹⁰They teach your ordinances to
    Jacob,
  your law to Israel.
They bring incense to your nostrils,
  and burnt offerings to your altar.
¹¹Bless, LORD, his strength,
  be pleased with the work of his
    hands.
Crush the loins of his adversaries
  and of his foes, that they may
    not rise.

MOSES' FOURTH ADDRESS

Deuteronomy 33:1–34:12

33:1-29 Blessing upon the tribes

The poem is a final eulogy to the ancient tribes. It is delimited by praise of the Lord (vv. 2-5, 26-29) and particularly the repetition of "Jeshurun," an obscure Hebrew name meaning "upright" (vv. 5, 26; see 32:15; Isa 44:2). This name is considered by some commentators to be a poetic term of endearment for Israel because of the similarity in sound between the names

¹²Of Benjamin he said:

> The beloved of the LORD,
> he abides in safety beside him;
> He shelters him all day long;
> the beloved abides at his breast.

¹³Of Joseph he said:

> Blessed by the LORD is his land
> with the best of heaven above
> and of the abyss crouching beneath;
> ¹⁴With the best of the produce of the sun,
> and the choicest yield of the months;
> ¹⁵With the finest gifts of the ancient mountains
> and the best from the everlasting hills;
> ¹⁶With the best of the earth and its fullness,
> and the favor of the one who dwells on Sinai.
> Let these come upon the head of Joseph
> and upon the brow of the prince among his brothers.
> ¹⁷His firstborn bull, majesty is his!
> His horns are the horns of a wild ox;
> With them he gores the peoples,
> attacks the ends of the earth.
> These are the myriads of Ephraim,
> and these the thousands of Manasseh.

¹⁸Of Zebulun he said:

> Rejoice, Zebulun, in your expeditions,
> exult, Issachar, in your tents!
> ¹⁹They invite peoples to the mountain
> where they offer right sacrifices,
> Because they suck up the abundance of the seas
> and the hidden treasures of the sand.

²⁰Of Gad he said:

> Blessed be the one who has made Gad so vast!
> He lies there like a lion;
> he tears the arm, the head as well.
> ²¹He saw that the best should be his,
> for there the commander's portion was assigned;
> he came at the head of the people.
> He carried out the justice of the LORD
> and his ordinances for Israel.

²²Of Dan he said:

> Dan is a lion's cub,
> that springs away from a viper!

²³Of Naphtali he said:

> Naphtali, abounding with favor,
> filled with the blessing of the LORD,
> take possession of the west and south.

Jacob, Israel, and Jerusalem in Hebrew. Curiously, Simeon is not included among the twelve tribes, and the number is balanced by Joseph praised as Ephraim and Manasseh.

Bodily imagery pervades the blessing; the Lord is present with hand and foot (vv. 3, 7), favor falls on the head and brow of Joseph (v. 16), and Gad seizes the arm and head of prey like a lion.

²⁴Of Asher he said:

> Most blessed of sons be Asher!
>> May he be the favorite among
>> his brothers,
>> and may he dip his foot in oil!
> ²⁵May the bolts of your gates be
>> iron and bronze;
>> may your strength endure
>> through all your days!

²⁶There is none like the God of
> Jeshurun,
>> who rides the heavens in his
>> power,
>> who rides the clouds in his
>> majesty;
²⁷The God of old is a refuge;
> a support are the arms of the
> Everlasting.
He drove the enemy out of your way
> and he said, "Destroy!"
²⁸Israel abides securely,
> Jacob dwells apart,
In a land of grain and wine,
> where the heavens drip with
> dew.
²⁹Happy are you, Israel! Who is like
> you,
> a people delivered by the LORD,
Your help and shield,
> and the sword of your glory.
Your enemies cringe before you;
> you stride upon their backs.

IV. THE DEATH OF MOSES

34 ¹Then Moses went up from the plains of Moab to Mount Nebo, the peak of Pisgah which faces Jericho, and the LORD showed him all the land— Gilead, and as far as Dan, ²all Naphtali, the land of Ephraim and Manasseh, all the land of Judah as far as the Western Sea, ³the Negeb, the plain (the valley of Jericho, the City of Palms), and as far as Zoar. ⁴The LORD then said to him, This is the land about which I promised on oath to Abraham, Isaac, and Jacob, "I will give it to your descendants." I have let you see it with your own eyes, but you shall not cross over. ⁵So there, in the land of Moab, Moses, the servant of the LORD, died as the LORD had said; ⁶and he was buried in a valley in the land of Moab, opposite Beth-peor; to this day no one knows the place of his burial. ⁷Moses was one hundred and twenty years old when he died, yet his eyes were undimmed and his vigor unabated. ⁸The Israelites wept for Moses in the plains of Moab for thirty days, till they had completed the period of grief and mourning for Moses.

⁹Now Joshua, son of Nun, was filled with the spirit of wisdom, since Moses

34:1-8 Death and burial of Moses

This section harks back to 3:23-29 and the denial of Moses' entry to the Promised Land. The book of Deuteronomy now comes full circle. The carefully cited geographical details speak to the cherished memory of Moses (1:1-5). Moses' burial site is unknown today. He is memorialized as a robust man who never succumbed to the vagaries of premature death and physical aging. He was blessed with divine favor in life and fondly remembered in death. Such a life is extolled in the psalms (Pss 39:5-8; 62:10; 128:5-6).

had laid his hands upon him; and so the Israelites gave him their obedience, just as the LORD had commanded Moses.

¹⁰Since then no prophet has arisen in Israel like Moses, whom the LORD knew face to face, ¹¹in all the signs and wonders the LORD sent him to perform in the land of Egypt against Pharaoh and all his servants and against all his land, ¹²and all the great might and the awesome power that Moses displayed in the sight of all Israel.

34:9-12 Praise of Joshua and Moses

Joshua is characterized as filled with the spirit of wisdom, a fitting gift from his mentor Moses. Wisdom is the gift of knowing how to live well in the world and attain the fullness of life. Sages are to teach their students well, as does Moses in the book of Deuteronomy.

Apart from the other models of Moses in the Scriptures (liberator, model of humility, judge, priest, and king), here his role as prophet is again accented. He is incomparable in his prophetic vocation. Like the classic Old Testament prophets, he serves the Lord in word and deed; he also suffers in his mission (Jer 37:15). His characterization in the Scriptures remains an abiding paradigm of service to the Lord, even amid the twists and turns of human frailty and sin.

These final verses in the book of Deuteronomy succinctly describe Moses. He performs signs and wonders before the Egyptian Pharaoh and manages to gain the trust of reluctant Hebrew slaves. At first a reluctant leader himself, he eventually comes into his own. In Deuteronomy his confidence shines.

The end of Deuteronomy is punctuated by the sixfold repetition of "all" (the Hebrew *kōl* is omitted in some translations). Moses is incomparable in *all* signs and wonders against Pharaoh and *all* his servants in *all* his land, as well as *all* the great might and *all* awesome power displayed before *all* Israel (vv. 11-12). The legacy of Moses is timeless.

To conclude, the book of Deuteronomy is both about the law and Moses the lawgiver. The book exhibits a complexity akin to human nature, i.e., nothing is simply two-dimensional; there are always contradictions and shadow sides. Hence, Deuteronomy exhorts care of the widow, orphan, resident alien, and Levite, while also presenting a plan of conquest that wipes out indigenous peoples. In the Ten Commandments wives are a separate category from other goods, but women are still in some sense a man's property. These and other realities offer material for reflection in the review aids and discussion topics below.

By New Testament times the role of Moses as the great lawgiver becomes paradigmatic. The canonical status of the torah in early Judaism makes Moses a key figure, and the New Testament gospels make clear parallels between Jesus and Moses. For example, Jesus' Sermon on the Mount mirrors Moses as lawgiver on Mount Sinai/Horeb. The Transfiguration places Jesus amidst Moses and Elijah, who were, respectively, the great lawgiver and the most esteemed prophet in Israel (Matt 17:1-8; Mark 9:2-8; Luke 9:28-36).

REVIEW AIDS AND DISCUSSION TOPICS

Introduction *(pages 5–8)*

1. Why is Deuteronomy an important Old Testament book and a key to our understanding of biblical tradition in both testaments?

2. Discuss the current state of opinion on the historical background and development of Deuteronomy. What are some opinions on its dating and the circles that produced it?

3. What are some aspects of the literary artistry of Deuteronomy? What literary devices inform this homily by Moses at the edge of the Promised Land?

1:1–4:43 Moses' first address *(pages 9–22)*

1. What information in the introduction to Deuteronomy (1:1-5) sets the stage for what follows?

2. What is the value of having others share leadership with Moses? How does this exhortation speak to the church today?

3. What are the key themes and motifs that run through the narrative and inform our understanding of the book's theological message?

4. Israel's conquest of the land in Deuteronomy is depicted as both peaceful and violent. What reasons are given for these differences? What current events come to mind regarding taking land from others? How might Deuteronomy inform our understanding of the moral issues surrounding warfare?

4:44–28:69 Moses' second address *(pages 22–90)*

1. Discuss the meaning and message of the Ten Commandments. What common themes and motifs run through them?

2. What are the key elements of the great Shema? How is this exhortation important for Israel's self-understanding and later Judeo-Christian tradition?

3. What attitudes and events embody the tension between blessing and curse in Deuteronomy? What values in Deuteronomy are essential for long life in the Promised Land?

4. Why does Deuteronomy repeat the theology of remembering/forgetting? What are the temptations of prosperity (8:1-20) that still speak to us today?

5. What does Deuteronomy teach about the theology of ecology? What themes and motifs speak to ecological concerns? What environmental attitudes in Deuteronomy seem no longer applicable in the modern world? What environmental attitudes remain timeless?

6. Describe the key aspects of true religion in Deuteronomy. What attitudes and practices underlie abomination and apostasy in Israel?

7. What do Deuteronomy and related biblical literature preach about teaching children and passing on the faith to the next generation? What challenges, both familial and communal, are involved in realizing these values?

8. What are the great Israelite feasts discussed in Deuteronomy? What aspects of Israelite worship continue to inform our worship today?

9. What does Deuteronomy teach about leadership in Israel, especially as embodied in the judge, king, priest, and prophet? What is characteristic of good leadership in any age?

10. What social justice values are modeled in Deuteronomy? How do care for the needy, commitment to family values, and the integrity of social interaction speak to justice and peace?

11. How do the Sea of Reeds and the Jordan River form a geographical connection between the exodus and entering the Promised Land?

29:1–32:52 Moses' third address *(pages 91–102)*

1. How does the theme of time inform our understanding of this address? What other biblical passages speak to the gift of time in the created order?

2. As Deuteronomy closes, the themes of decision and choice are offered. How are these themes applicable to current events in the church? In your own life?

3. How does Deuteronomy portray the legacy of Moses?

4. What are the major themes and motifs in the Song of Moses (32:1-43)? Compare this song with other poetry in Deuteronomy and elsewhere in the Old Testament.

33:1–34:12 Moses' fourth address *(pages 103–107)*

1. How does Deuteronomy characterize the transfer of leadership from Moses to Joshua?

2. What is the overall Deuteronomic portrait of Moses?

INDEX OF CITATIONS FROM THE
CATECHISM OF THE CATHOLIC CHURCH

The arabic number(s) following the citation refer(s) to the paragraph number(s) in the *Catechism of the Catholic Church*. The asterisk following a paragraph number indicates that the citation has been paraphrased.

Deuteronomy					
1-11	708*	5:19	2400, 2450	15:11	2449
4:13	2056	5:21	2533	18:10	2116*
4:15-16	2129	5:22	2056, 2058	24:1	1610*
4:19	57*	6:4-5	201, 459,* 2093*	24:14-15	1867,* 2409,*
4:37	218*	6:4	228, 2083		2434*
5:2	2060	6:5	368,* 2055,* 2133	25:13-16	2409*
5:4	2059	6:13-14	2084	28:10	63
5:6-22	2056*	6:13	2096, 2150	29–30	708*
5:6-9	2083*	6:16	2119	29:3	368*
5:6	431, 2061, 2133	7:6	762*	30:15-20	1696*
5:11	2141	7:8	218*	30:16	2057
5:12-15	2167*	7:9	215*	31:9	2056*
5:12	2189	8:3	1334,* 2835	31:24	2056*
5:15	2057, 2170	10:4	2056*	32:6	238*
5:16	2196,* 2200, 2247	10:15	218*	32:8	57,* 441*
5:17	2330	11:14	1293*	32:34	1295*
		14:1	441*	32:39	304*

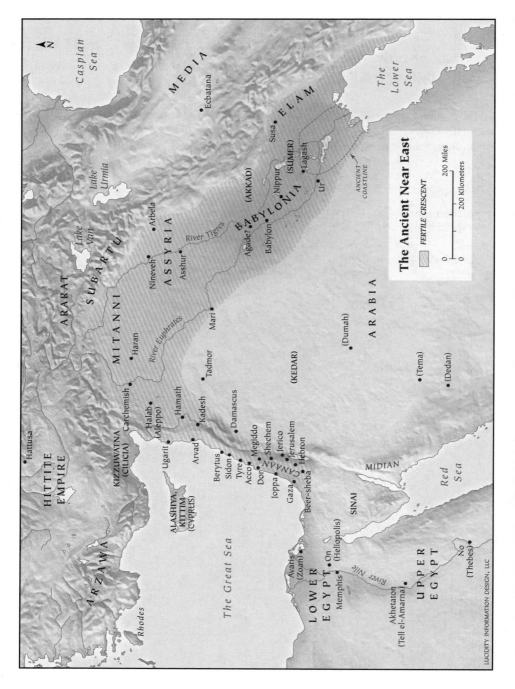

The Ancient Near East

FERTILE CRESCENT

0   200 Miles
0   200 Kilometers

LUCIDITY INFORMATION DESIGN, LLC